LETTERS TO POSEIDON

Also by Cees Nooteboom in English translation

FICTION
Rituals
Philip and the Others
The Following Story
The Knight Has Died
A Song of Truth and Semblance
Mokusei
All Souls' Day
Lost Paradise
The Foxes Come at Night

NON-FICTION
Roads to Santiago
Nomad's Hotel
Roads to Berlin

POETRY
Self-portrait of an Other

CEES NOOTEBOOM

LETTERS TO POSEIDON

PREFACE BY
ALBERTO MANGUEL

Translated from the Dutch by
Laura Watkinson

MacLehose Press
New York • London

MacLehose Press
An imprint of Quercus
New York • London

First published in the Dutch language as *Brieven aan Poseidon*
by Uitgeverij de Bezige Bij, Amsterdam, in 2012

Copyright © Cees Nooteboom 2012
English translation copyright © 2014 by Laura Watkinson
Preface © Alberto Manguel
English translation copyright of preface © Anna Milsom
First published in the United States by Quercus in 2015

The publisher gratefully acknowledges the support of the Dutch Foundation
for Literature.

N ederlands
letterenfonds
dutch foundation
for literature

ISBN 978-1-62365-914-1

Library of Congress control number: 2015954547

Distributed in the United States and Canada by
Hachette Book Group
1290 Avenue of the Americas
New York, NY 10104

Manufactured in the United States

10 9 8 7 6 5 4 3 2 1

www.quercus.com

For Siegfried Unseld,
who changed so much for me

The death of one god is the death of all.

WALLACE STEVENS

CONTENTS

PREFACE XIII
LETTERS TO POSEIDON 1
Poseidon I 5
Married to a Hat 7
Siege 8
Bayreuth 10
Poseidon II 11
Encounter 13
Invalides 14
Poseidon III 15
River 17
Challenger 20
Poseidon IV 21
Asclepias 23
Time 24
Poseidon V 25
Lorry 27
Kenkō 28
Telephone 30
Poseidon VI 32
Infanticide 33
Books 35

Poseidon VII   37
Wall   40
Blur   42
Poseidon VIII   44
Hölderlin   46
Veils   48
Painting   50
Poseidon IX   52
Orion   55
Pastorale   58
Poseidon X   59
Conversation   62
Agave   63
Poseidon XI   66
Walk   69
Witness   71
Poseidon XII   73
Chair   75
Donkeys   78
Garden   80
Poseidon XIII   82
Girl   85
Blood Moon   87
Poseidon XIV   90
Man   92
Surface   94
Green   95
Poseidon XV   97
Bal Des Ambassadeurs   101
Circe   103
Harbour   105
Poseidon XVI   108

Hippopotamus 111

Hesiod 113

Poseidon XVII 116

Quilotoa 118

Thunderstorm 121

Zoo 123

Poseidon XVIII 126

Lives 129

Bull 132

Poseidon XIX 134

Sisters 136

Whale 138

Blue 141

Poseidon XX 143

War 146

Ratón 149

Posidonia 151

Poseidon XXI 154

Old 157

Flame 160

Poseidon XXII 164

Colleagues 168

Stone 171

Poseidon XXIII 174

Notes and Illustrations 177

Acknowledgements 235

Picture Credits 237

PREFACE

Cees Nooteboom is one of those writers, like Montaigne, Hazlitt and Borges, who make us feel more intelligent. It is not that his books are didactic or erudite. On the contrary, approximation and doubt are part of his style. His tone is one of astonished assurance, not arrogant instruction, of inquisitive perplexity, never pedantic certainty. It is as if the world for Nooteboom were a text made up of marvellous metaphors that do not allow for translation into any language at all, just humble recognition, and our task is to journey through with our eyes wide open. In this sense, in his essays as in his fiction and poetry, Nooteboom has always been a writer of travel books.

Letters to Poseidon is a kind of notebook documenting one such journey. The title is justified by the intention to direct a series of messages and observations from the present to one of the great gods of antiquity, initiating a dialogue not only with the past, but with an entire world that seemed lost for ever. The god, who for Kafka (the author notes) no longer even saw the oceans he administered from behind a bureaucratic desk, is for Nooteboom the recipient of rhetorical questions, slivers of experience, snapshots that the journeys and the days bring to him like salvaged *objets-trouvés*. "Forgetting is the absent brother of Memory," writes Nooteboom. Nooteboom feeds the one with the phantoms of the other.

Writing letters to those who are no longer of this world is an ancient literary form. According to Diodorus Siculus, the Egyptians used to write to deceased relatives "so they might live again"; almost three thousand years later, Walter Savage Landor composed his *Imaginary Conversations* choosing Dante, Aesop, Calvin and others from among the famous dead as correspondents. Theology provides wonderful examples of correspondence with the God who died on the cross, but only Nooteboom has dared to write to a god who preceded Him, a god "from an age before writing."

Twenty-three letters and a series of notes (postcards, we might call them) are directed, not without startling hubris, to the vengeful deity who forced Ulysses into his odyssey and owes his name (according to Socrates, Nooteboom tells us) to a man who experienced the sea as shackles (*desmos*) binding his feet (*podōn*). The god Poseidon, Nooteboom confesses, attracts him like something from "a world before history."

Nooteboom subjects this neglected god to questions that have no answers, or only answers that form a part of the question itself and cannot be resolved according to logical syntax. These are questions which are, as is proper when dealing with gods, sufficient unto themselves: "What is a human being to the gods?"; "Is there a hierarchy in the kingdom of the dead?"; "Is a person who has been dead for a few thousand years as dead as someone who died last year?"; "Do gods read?"; "For how long can a person look at a stone?"; "Can seaweed also be a memento mori?"; "[W]hat is more of a mystery? Someone who is able to die, or someone who is never permitted to die?"; "[W]hich god will appear when the barbarians come?"

Perhaps the key to the book is to be found in one of its shortest texts, "Lorry." After describing the innocuous-looking newspaper photograph of a parked vehicle, Nooteboom explains that it depicts the scene of a tragedy, where a girl was murdered and her stepfather found hanged from a tree. No-one can say exactly what happened, or why. Nooteboom writes: "The dead are silent, leaving behind a mystery in the shape of a big lorry beside a few trees." And later, casually: "The most likely scenario is that the incident was connected to some impossible form of love." The supposed explanation reveals all and explains nothing. It is a story with "no solution, no mercy, life as its own punishment," as he says elsewhere.

Dante, invoked several times by Nooteboom in the book, believed that all of our crimes were the product of love, either excessive (avarice, lust) or insufficient (anger, envy). In "Challenger" Nooteboom goes further: he suggests that this same love offers an instrument which allows us to see the world in all its fractured unity: to recognise, for example, in a space-shuttle disaster, the explosion of the *Challenger*, a kaleidoscopic vision of the universe, "a cloud, made up of powdered flesh and metal, finely pulverised existences, living and dead matter that has assumed the form of a hazy white cloud, a grave of dust becoming finer and finer as it fans out, the infinite disintegration of bodies of men and women who once had names."

In one of these letters, Nooteboom asks Poseidon who his "one last supplicant" might be. We know the answer to that question: a nomadic Dutchman, a clear-sighted optimist, an inveterate inquisitor, one of the best writers of this disillusioned century.

ALBERTO MANGUEL

LETTERS TO POSEIDON

How does something begin? 2008, a February day in Munich. On Marienplatz I buy a book by Sándor Márai, not a novel, but short pieces. It is called *Die vier Jahreszeiten* and it looks a little mournful: a snapped stem, a large flower hanging down, its petals still shut tight, and yet already slightly wilting, a melancholy image that seems out of place on this unexpectedly sunny day in the heart of winter. Years ago, before anyone was talking about Márai, Klaus Bittner gave me the writer's last diary in Cologne, bitter, sparse pages, notes written in the years leading up to his suicide at the age of eighty-eight. Exile in San Diego. Why San Diego, for heaven's sake? I know that city. How does a Hungarian cosmopolitan finish up there, at the end of a life, with a gunshot the final sound? His wife, with whom he had spent a lifetime travelling, has become ill. He visits her at the nursing home, she dies, and her ashes are scattered at sea. He lives on, alone, an uphill struggle, reading Aristotle, the diary becoming painful, fragmentary. And then comes death. He will not live to see his great—posthumous—success. My Hungarian friends are surprised at the enthusiastic reaction to his novels. They prefer his diaries, his travel writing. He was a bright presence in a long, dark century of fascism and communism, of constantly shifting borders.

I walk to Viktualienmarkt with my new book and look for a place to read. People are sitting outside, and I spot a free table outside a fish restaurant. I order a glass of champagne to celebrate the first day of spring, and I begin to read. The book was published in 1938, but what I am reading is the work of a contemporary, a man who spends his life looking and reading, travelling and writing. I had simply sat down where I had found a free chair, but the paper napkin I am given has the name POSEIDON written on it in letters that are the same blue as the sea I live beside in the summer. It must be a sign, someone wants to tell me something, and I have learned to heed such signs. The god is depicted with his trident, and, even though I am in the middle of writing a book, I decide that I shall start writing letters to him as soon as that book is finished—small collections of words, reports from my life.

The German winter becomes a Spanish summer, my book is done, and, in the emptiness that inevitably follows, I remember that sunny winter's day of six months ago. In three days' time, my seventy-sixth year will begin. The day after that is the start of the month of August, the emperor's month. I have never written to a god before.

Evening is falling on the island, the sea is close, Poseidon's sea, the rocks where I always swim. I look out at the vast, gently rippling surface, the movement in the last gleam of sunlight. The water on the rocks is the only sound. I simply need to begin.

POSEIDON I

In a relief that dates back to somewhere around the birth of Christ, who supplanted you, and whom we use to divide endless time in two, the twelve Olympian gods stand in a long line. They have their attributes with them, but their destination is unclear. Apollo, Artemis, Zeus, Athene. Then you. You are the first of the gods to look back, but Hera behind you, still so young, has closed her eyes, and is not returning your gaze. What were you looking at? Your left hand rests on your right side, while your right hand loosely holds your trident, that curious weapon by which we can always identify you. You used it for fishing, and every fish belonged to you. All of you are standing side on, Assyrian, Babylonian, that is how you appear, as if your bodies could not yet let go of the stone. That was at a time when we could not yet let go of you. Why did I choose you? Because I spend part of the year beside your sea? Because, before I head north again at the beginning of autumn, I always swim out from the rocks at the same place, even in rain or stormy weather? I do so in order to ask if I may return next year, and who should I ask but you? I had been looking for someone to write to for a long time, but how does a man write letters to a god? It is very simple—we do not, and yet I am doing it all the same. In a roundabout way. Leave what you write on the beach, on a rock by the sea, and hope that he will find it. My letters will be about things that I read, that I see, that I think. That I make up, that I remember, that surprise me. Reports from the world, like the one about the man who married a dead woman. Perhaps you will find them, perhaps they will blow away. I am writing them because I thought you might want to hear something about the world. I do not know what will happen next. I never know. All I can do is imagine. Receiving a reply was never the point. I have always wondered how it felt when no-one prayed to you any longer, and no-one asked anything of you. There must, once upon a time, have been one last supplicant. Who was it? And where? Did you and the other gods talk about it? We look at your statues, but you are not there. Were you jealous of the gods who came after you? Are you laughing now that they too have been abandoned?

MARRIED TO A HAT

In a small village in the south of France, a 68-year-old Frenchman has married a woman who has no age, because she is dead. They had lived together for twenty years and intended to marry, but she became ill and died. The man took the dead woman's hat to the wedding, for which the French president had granted his permission. The hero of Gustav Meyrink's *The Golem* has the thoughts of the man whose hat he is wearing. What was the woman's hat thinking on her wedding day? There were dozens of guests. Did the hat recognise them? And what did it say to the man when they were alone at home again, just the two of them?

SIEGE

At the Prado, in one of the galleries upstairs in the new extension. A painting by Pieter Snayers. There are no other visitors, so the silence pervading this work has an even stronger impact. In the city where I am now standing, it is almost forty degrees outside, but inside the painting it has snowed, and I can feel that snow beneath my feet. The year is 1641. We are Spaniards, our war with France has been going on for six years and will continue for another eighteen. We are on a high hill, looking out over the plain below and upon the town centre and walls of Aire-sur-la-Lys. Our gaze extends to the horizon, a low strip of bluish land with, above it, the northerly light and those clouds, as seen only in these distant parts. Our own language sounds strange in these surroundings, a few bare trees around us, a couple of dogs. We must recapture the town and we will do so. That is what the history books say. To the left, beneath us, the troops in those unreal minutes of silence that precede every battle. Below them, the unseen enemy lies in wait. A man who looks at us one day, later, will, for a moment, lift our nameless selves up out of death, but our thoughts on that day we will keep to ourselves. What he will see is history, or art, or both. But he will know nothing about the breath that came from our mouths that morning, nothing about the sound of the crows, or the hoofs of the horses on the frozen ground.

BAYREUTH

It happens every summer, as surely as Wimbledon and the Tour de France. German sounds come wafting into my Mediterranean garden. They are still unsure, not knowing if they are welcome. Brass instruments, loud, high-pitched voices, timpani. They seem to be exploring the surroundings. I can feel that everything in my garden is on the alert, is resisting. The palms, the hibiscus, the cacti, the papyrus, plants that would perish in the cold mists of the North. But this music knows no mercy, and revels in its power. I hear those sustained Germanic notes, the military sound of the choir, the bite of that other language, the hunting blasts of the horns, the swelling of a large orchestra, the betrayal of Tristan, who will deliver Isolde to his king, her fury, the cries of grief, disguised as song, that tear past the pale lilac of the plumbago, and race through the bougainvillea like a sudden storm, leaving splashes of purple on the ground. I sit in the midst of it all, homeless, uprooted, a northern gardener beneath the oleasters, captive within the contradiction of my life.

POSEIDON II

You are a god, and I am a man. That is, however one looks at it, the state of affairs. But perhaps I might be permitted to ask you something I have always wanted to know. What is a human being to the gods? Do you despise us for being mortal? Or is the opposite the case? Are you jealous because we are allowed to die? Because your fate is, of course, immortality, even though we have no idea where you are now.

No-one talks about you anymore, and perhaps that hurts. It is as if you have simply vanished.

And yet, if it is true that you are immortal, and I assume that it is, then you must always remain. The end of the world, which you foretold, has not yet come. Have you gods stayed close to your empty temples? Did you become addicted to the sacrifices we made? Do you miss us, long for us? For a time we are the image of you, until we collapse, becoming ruins that can still think, still speak. Then we no longer resemble you.

But what is more of a mystery? Someone who is able to die, or someone who is never permitted to die? And so I return to my first question: what do the gods actually think of us?

Went down to the sea today, in a gale. Sat on a rock for a long time, looking out at the waves, so grey and wild. No answer, of course not. You sometimes disguised yourselves as humans, so that you could say something to us. At times I think you still do, that I have met one of you. But I will never know for sure.

ENCOUNTER

Two boys walk towards me on the narrow path from the sea to the village.

One is an adolescent, tall, unformed, everything about his body swings to and fro. This makes the steps of the much smaller boy behind him appear far more thoughtful. Dark, southern, Roman. His age is hard to guess, perhaps nine or ten, but what strikes me is the inward focus of his gaze. Of course I have no way of knowing what he sees there, but the mystery of that extreme concentration sends me reeling back through time. How long is it since I was that age? Why does something about it seem familiar? Was the man I am now, almost seventy years later, already present in the child I do not remember? That puzzle stays with me for the rest of the day. Can that happen, another person serving as a mirror in which one's own age evaporates? Why do I believe I have encountered myself? And if I have not, then who is it that I met, but will never know?

INVALIDES

The dead here are forever invalids. They will never move again. Their ten coffins are arrayed in ceremonial symmetry with the classical edifice in the distance. There is a lot of space between the building and the coffins. In the photograph, that space looks white, as if it has snowed. A single, central figure stands at the middle point: the president of France. He has brought home the dead. What cannot be seen in the photograph is the unasked question: what kind of war is this? The distance makes it impossible to see any facial expressions, and so the dramaturgy of the number prevails: one facing many. Napoleon built this Dôme for his soldiers; at this moment thoughts of him are not far away. The act of capturing the sentiment of mourning in a geometry of theatrical purity has its own pathos. Diagonally behind the president a man is saluting. His rank is invisible at this distance. The soldiers lined up in front of the building, along both sides and next to the coffins, form a pentagon, a classical diagram. There must have been sound, but in this picture only silence reigns.

POSEIDON III

Today I read a piece by Kafka that I had not come across before. It bears your name: Poseidon.

Kafka is a continent; when you read him, you always end up in places you have never been. So if we can assume that some literature is timeless, then you are still alive, but apparently you are not happy. I cannot see you taking part in a procession of gods without feeling the need to correct the image, as I know you do not have enough time for that sort of thing. Too busy. According to Kafka, you never actually saw the sea from above, or only occasionally, on your rare ascents of Mount Olympus. The sea lay there, far beneath you, large, grey and shifting. That last part is not in the story; those words are mine. The mountain on the island where I live is not as high as Olympus, but once a year I climb it and look out at the sea. Large, grey and shifting, as I said. You remain beneath the waves, and so you do not actually know the element over which you rule. I am not sure what to make of that. A tired god under the water, that is how Kafka sees you. Beneath a transparent, moving ceiling. Restless. Someone who is always making calculations, who is responsible for the management of all the waters. You have to keep on doing the job, because they do not have anyone else. Kafka does not say who "they" are, but that is what makes him Kafka. It is a sad image. An old man at a desk, who just keeps on working away, deep beneath the water's surface. Out of a sense of duty. Forget about the trident; in fact, those stories about you travelling the waters, trident in hand, are what annoy you most. Not a word about water nymphs or mermaids. Apparently you are waiting for the world to end. Just before then, when you have balanced the books, you might go for a quick boat tour, says Kafka. A tour . . . How am I ever going to shake off that thought?

RIVER

Leticia. A muddy slope descends to the river. People, pigs, dogs, all milling around together. Down by the water, slim boats with rowers to take people across to the other side, to the little island called Fantasia. Behind me, the market, the fruit, the fish. Someone helps me down the slippery slope to the jetty where the motorboats moor. The others are already there. Three Colombians from Cali, two Dutch. Two boatmen who will take us a hundred kilometres upstream. One of them sits up front, and I take my place beside the other, who is steering. As soon as we leave the shore, the river seems to open up, a vista of sparkling, metallic water between low banks that move further and further apart.

The little boat slices open the river, the shrill sound at odds with the immeasurable silence that must usually hold sway out here in the middle of this wide stretch of water. We stop at the Amacayacu nature park: a path plotted in the rainforest, planks over the boggy ground, the orgiastic glow of a thousand shades of green, leaves from a twisted dream, knives, serrated and sharp, a pond of rotting water plants beneath a sky that is growing darker and darker, the distant growl of a large storm. A monkey in make-up sits down beside me and looks at me as if it wants to enter into a discussion about proofs for the existence of God, but then the rain comes, not falling, but standing upright, a grey, almost opaque screen of water, and when it stops, the ground starts to steam as if the mud is boiling. The light is now made of zinc and iron, and as we set off again it hurts our eyes. We will see pink dolphins dancing alongside us and clouds constantly changing shape. The river is thousands of kilometres long, and I should like to sail onwards to Iquitos, and as far as the Andes. The sound of the engine is intoxicating, we encounter hardly anyone, only now and then one of those low boats occupied by slender figures, the same riverbanks for hours on end, green, green, and the riddles of the life that unfolds in this world without roads or cars, until, hours later, we turn around and sail back with the current to the island of Santa Rosa, in Peru. The ground is mud, trees with interlacing aerial roots, a bare tree full of vultures nearby, wooden houses on stilts, a group of women in a semi-circle. There are about a dozen of them, and each has an animal in her arms: a sloth, a parrot, an alligator, a young crocodile, a turtle, an iguana, a giant frog. This has obviously been arranged, what these women are doing is a job, and later the driver of the boat will ask us for a financial contribution. A lone man sits to one side of the women. He has a small kind of jaguar on a rope, it hisses as soon as I approach. Our small party of travellers stands in front of the women, looking at the animals, an absurdist scene: the queen on a working visit. The women are of various ages; they are wearing T-shirts and shorts. What they are thinking cannot be read on their faces. Or on ours, I think to myself. You don't stroke a crocodile, the sloth appears to be fast asleep, and the turtle is two hundred years old and already knows everything there is to know. I walk away from the group across a sandy field to a wooden building painted in pink and pale green: Asamblea Tradicional de Dios, Iglesia Evangélica. The gods are never far away. I walk up the rickety stairs and inside, into a large, empty room. At the other end is a kind of altar with a lectern for the Word, behind it are five bright-green plastic chairs, and in front of it are six narrow wooden benches with no backrests. Light shines in through the chinks and cracks in the wooden walls. It is peaceful there, quiet. Where people pray often, the divine reigns, said the philosopher who himself did not believe in God. For a moment I stand in that silence, and then I hear the boat's engine starting up. As we move off, I watch the group on the bank swiftly fading into invisibility until finally they vanish into the distant green of the riverbank, as if a drawing were being erased: a village on an island in the river on the border between Peru, Colombia and Brazil, an endless distance from the capital city of Lima, where nobody knows its name.

CHALLENGER

It is not an animal, even though there appears to be a head with a misty eye at the top right, two limp, bewildered horns of swirling dust, a few long, white, pointed whiskers, a thin and unsteady neck, a patch of darker fur just above. A challenger, but what or whom was it challenging? The black shroud of the universe, beyond?

But this is not an animal. It is a cloud, made up of powdered flesh and metal, finely pulverised existences, living and dead matter that has assumed the form of a hazy white cloud, a grave of dust becoming finer and finer as it fans out, the infinite disintegration of bodies of men and women who once had names.

POSEIDON IV

I do not know if you ever read what is written about you.
Homer, Kafka, Ovid? Probably not. But that is how I know
more about you than you think, and all of it raises questions. Kafka calls you Poseidon, while Ovid calls you Neptune. I shall admit it: I do not like your Latin name. It is just
like a writer with a pseudonym; there has to be a good reason for it. Either you must become your pseudonym, like
Stendhal, or you divide yourself over all kinds of different
names, like Pessoa, each name ruling out another, perhaps
even killing it. Neptune was never able to defeat Poseidon,
not for me. It is Poseidon who stands in the market square
in Lindau, not Neptune. He carries the same trident, but
still he is an impostor, someone impersonating you, who
has taken everything about you that is Greek and covered
it with a layer of Rome. Dante did not read Greek; he calls
you Neptune, but I know that it is you. *Paradiso* XXXIII,
the final book of the *Commedia*, where the poet stands
in the eternal light of an indescribable vision and knows he
has gazed into the depths of the divine mystery, the unity
of all existence, and yet still he wishes to describe it. He
realises that he will never be able to hold on to the memory

of what he has seen, because he is only a man, and that this memory shall slip away from him, just as you, through the mists of twenty-five centuries, have forgotten that wondrous moment when you once saw the shadow of the *Argo* passing overhead. You were startled by the sight, writes Dante, and I try to imagine that moment, a god who had never before seen a ship on any of his oceans, a mysterious shadow sailing by with the unfamiliar billow of a sail, an elongated object populated by rowers, the sudden sound of human voices, a king as captain, mortal hunters in search of the Golden Fleece.

ASCLEPIAS

On November 14, 1827, the Duchess of Duras wrote to Chateaubriand: "My former life is so far removed from my present life that I feel as if I am reading a memoir, or watching a play." Two months later, she died in Nice. She read, without reading, the memoirs of her own life that he had written in his memoirs. So what I am reading is a doubling of memories. This is nothing to be surprised about. Two aristocratic individuals who could both write well, and who lived in a turbulent era. Terror, emigration, restoration. Big themes, and yet it is something else that has caught my attention. In that same letter she writes that she has sent him an "*asclepias carnata*," a laurel-like climbing plant that does not fear the cold, and which has a flower as red as the camellia. Plant it beneath the windows of the Benedictine's library, she says. The Benedictine was her name for him. The writer as monk. The magic of reading. A dead duchess, a dead writer, the route the plant travels from Nice to Lausanne, its arrival at the library. What I see is the red of that flower, and I can see it now.

TIME

My watch is a flat rectangle with a double, but very thin, gold edge. If it is true that it represents an aspect of time, then time keeps a very low profile on my wrist. The question is whether time also exists outside that gold surround. Its face is white, and the brown of summer makes that immobile white stand out sharply against my living skin. The numbers are Roman, the IV and the VIII are angled downwards, the VI stands on its head, upside down, time having tripped into its own trap. Near that number is a word written so small that I need a magnifying glass to read it. When I enlarge the letters, I see, for the first time in thirty years, that it says "Quartz." No-one knows for certain where that word comes from. It connects me to the mineral world. Flint, granite, amethyst. The IX and the III are opposite points standing in exemplary equilibrium on an imaginary horizon. So that cannot be the cause of my dismay. I must have dropped my watch at some point. A thin, jagged fault line runs across the glass above that white face with its symmetrical numbers, disrupting the order of time. If that can happen on my wrist, then why not everywhere else?

POSEIDON V

Every pure form, that is to say every form that is not mixed with matter, is an intelligence, a sentence from a medieval Arab philosopher. Do such abstractions mean something to you? Did your philosophers, by which I mean the thinkers who lived alongside contemporaries who were still worshipping you, ever really devote their thoughts to you and your fellow gods? Or were they already more interested in the One, other god, who was not connected to a particular natural phenomenon or human activity, not responsible for fire, or war, or love? What did you gods think of that One, whom we could not imagine as a human being, while attempting to do exactly that? We had made him into an elderly man so as to give ourselves something to hold on to, perhaps because we missed you, but over time He became more ethereal, more invisible and, if one can put it this way, less human, an idea and yet also someone who, unlike you and your fellows, never really concerned Himself with us, even though the priests said He did. In the end, He died, or at least one of his three forms did, but what interests me is what you Olympians thought of Him. Did you find your competitor just as enigmatic as most mortals do? Someone who never replied when you asked Him something, but who had written a Book that said He had created everything. He did not bother Himself with details such as simple natural phenomena, He was there only for the very greatest kinds of violence, like the Great Flood, when the whole world was threatened. After all, He had you and your fellows for such things as thunder and lightning. But that was the problem; you did not appear in His book, unless it was as idols and false gods. False people do not exist, not in that sense, but false gods do, and in His Book, he is furious with jealousy of you. Why is that? Was that one of the reasons for your downfall?

Should he not have been aware that most people are unable to deal with abstractions? He could have made better use of you. Later, when He had already lived for an infinite length of time, He had a Son who was also human, rather like you Olympians, and yet different, because unlike you this god could die, but only as a human. That moment formed a hiatus in time, and from then on your calendar no longer applied. I do not know if you still pay attention to our actions, or if such things still interest you. Sometimes when the wind here suddenly bends all the trees at the same time, like drunken servants, or when the sea screams its rage at the rocks and the sky is a page covered with white electric writing, I think you and the other gods must be somewhere nearby, but no-one ever sees you anymore.

LORRY

A photograph in *The Times*. A lorry. It is parked on the roadside next to some trees. Someone might walk past and think, look, a lorry, but maybe not even that. Large, solid; the men who drive these vehicles are strong. The driver left home at three in the morning; lorry-drivers work long hours. His nine-year-old stepdaughter went with him. Her mother later said there was absolutely no reason for her not to have allowed her daughter to go with her husband. The lorry was parked in that one place for a while, so someone went to take a look. The girl was dead inside the cab, murdered. There was no sign of the man, so they combed the area. He was found in a nearby wood, hanging from a tree. No signs of sexual assault were found on the girl. The dead are silent, leaving behind a mystery in the shape of a big lorry beside a few trees. What happened? The most likely scenario is that the incident was connected to some impossible form of love that led inevitably to this double death. I take another look at the photograph. The lorry, which looks like a lorry, is loaded with such an intense charge that it is almost impossible to bear.

KENKŌ

How to describe a Japanese drawing that is not particularly good? Perhaps by trying to make clear just how very
askew it is. A simple bamboo house slides from top left to
bottom right. The drawing is black and white, done in thin
pen strokes. The thatched roof is just some lightly drawn
lines, the lake a few meandering lines in the water, with
some scribbles in the lazy mountains serving as vegetation.
A twisted pine to the left of the house, a blossoming cherry
tree to the right, a stream below, and a few strokes of the
pen suggesting the rush of the water. No sun, no moon, as
the artist needed the empty sky for a poem. The words that
he drew can fly, dancing upright against the white. There is
nothing finer than sitting all alone beneath a lamp, a book
spread out on the desk in front of you, and making friends
with people you have never met, people from a distant age.
That is what those sentences say, those graceful garlands in
the empty sky. A rock, a bush, a barrel, a bamboo fence,
an alcove, a sliding panel made of rice paper—this is the
universe of the reading philosopher. Was it Kenkō himself,
drawn by Sukenobu? Kenkō wrote his *Tsurezuregusa* in
the fourteenth century. Essays about idleness. The drawing

was made four centuries later. The monk's big bald head rests on his left hand, the book is open in front of him, and his writing materials are beside him, but he will not start writing until later; right now he is either reading or thinking about what he has read. He is sitting very still. Perhaps he can hear the water, perhaps the wind in the pine tree. Soon, when he writes something down, it will appear in the book that is here on my desk seven centuries later: *Essays in Idleness: The Tsurezuregusa of Kenkō*.

TELEPHONE

A Dutchman on a Spanish island and an American woman in Dublin talk on the telephone. There are seven billion people in the world, so these two individuals speaking to each other might seem like an extreme coincidence. But, as the philosopher rightly said, all that is real is rational. Both have made a career of writing, and they met at a literary festival. Since then, the two have moved all over the world and they talk and write to each other every now and then. Yesterday's conversation—across the Pyrenees, across the Irish Sea—was about what they were reading at that moment. She was reading a biography of Nureyev; he Volume III of Chateaubriand's *Mémoires d'outre-tombe*. Could it have been the other way around? That is unlikely. He is not particularly interested in dance; she would probably not be too enthusiastic about the detailed report penned by Ambassador Chateaubriand to his ministry about the possibility of a European conflict between Turkey, Austria, Russia, Prussia and England, and the role that France might play. The man in Spain is reading it not so much for the politics and the history, but for Chateaubriand's magnificent, concise French, in which he analyses European relationships like a game of chess. She, in Dublin, has read the 782 pages of Julie Kavanagh's "beautifully written" biography deep into the night. Both have penetrated, at a particular point and a particular moment, into the endless series of manifestations of our existence on earth, and are reporting back to each other. There is nothing remarkable about that, and yet there is.

POSEIDON VI

Perhaps my shortest letter. Legends of the world—that is what I am sending to you. *Legenda*, what is to be read. *Quod legendum est*. Perhaps. Flashes, stories, histories, anecdotes in search of the aura of legend. Parvenus from the morning newspaper with a desire for longevity, seeking marble and parchment. Every day a Trojan War, not yet refined by any poet, every day a king without a number, a general with an army of only one soldier, anonymous lives with the fame of one single day, lives that I offer up to you, as I am the only one who is writing to you. I know that you know everything already, but only in the language of the gods. That will not help you to fathom us. Have you ever understood anything about human beings? Or does our mortality make us inaudible? As I am writing to you, I am listening to music written by a centenarian. Mosaic. Dialogues. Enchanted preludes. "Scrivo in Vento," I write in the wind. We cannot come any closer to immortality than that. It is a taste that you Olympians do not know. The pain of time, our greatest asset. Rust, decay, mould that turns into music, something different from your eternal nectar. The final tally of our days, a gift no-one can take from us.

INFANTICIDE

I know the place where it happened, a small town on a big lake where three countries meet. At that time of year, all of those lands are covered in snow. The town is situated in a wide circle of mountains; sometimes nature has to become the indifferent backdrop to a drama in which people are destroyed. The same is true of the sky, an ashen grey-black on that day, growing darker still as the mother of the murdered child heads off to her job at a restaurant. She leaves her two sons in the care of a young man. The boys are three and six years old. The younger one is called Cain, the other has no name in the story, and this particular Cain is not an offender, but the victim. His nameless brother is present when Cain is kicked and beaten to death. Who would call their child Cain? That only becomes possible when a name no longer means what it once meant, when the evil associations that cling to that name have fallen into obscurity. And what about the evil itself? Evil is present in all times and places, but is it possible that its tone is different in this era? In Homer, fury was connected to a sense of honour. Achilles' dignity, and therefore his honour, is wounded. The *Iliad* begins with the consequences of his terrible wrath.

Wrath, a word that is slowly slipping from my vocabulary. It always means something when words disappear. What kind of wrath is involved in the case of Cain's murderer? Can the killer appeal to the glamour of myth, which grows stronger over time? Will his deed ever become anything other than foul mud, worth only a scream in black and red on the front page of a tabloid?

Augustine writes in his *Confessions* about the attraction of the gory gladiator fights and mutilated corpses at the Coliseum. Our eyes draw us, he says, to the sight of violence. Did myths provide a pretext for evil in Greek antiquity? Kronos killing and eating his children, Atreus murdering and cooking the sons of Thyestes, Thyestes unwittingly eating them. If transcendence lends another dimension to evil, must hexameters, poets, gods and kings be deployed, in this age without magic, so as to outdo the gutter press?

The town where this took place lay there yesterday, between the water and the mountains, as if nothing had happened. I walked through the park, along the water, in a still, late light. The smooth surface rested beneath a gentle mist, a boat with a fisherman, and in the distance the lights of the other country.

What captured my attention was the simultaneity. The man beating a child to death, a scene the other child will never forget, while the mother remains unaware. What kind of moment is that? Not the voice of the messenger of ill tidings in Epidaurus, not the mother's cry amidst the silence of those watching, not the chorus' words of mourning as they offer up this incident to the absent gods, no purification, no catharsis, only the bile of circulation figures, and an escape to the rest of the news.

BOOKS

The situation is unclear. A table in flowing water. If the size of the legs is normal, the water cannot be deep. A wide stream, or a flood. You can see from the small waves and ripples that it is flowing quickly. Behind the table is something resembling a riverbank, with a dark backdrop beyond, a rock face or a slope covered in undergrowth. The table is made of metal, with surface and legs in the same gleaming material, modern, all very familiar. It is simply that it does not belong in the water, and certainly not with books on it. There are no other people around, I am the only one here.

I cannot see what kind of books they are, they are closed, all I can make out from where I am standing are the bottom edges of the pages. No spines, no lettering. They are not new, these books. They have been stacked up, but in a disorderly way. If they stay there too long, they will get damp. Whose are they? Who left them there?

They could be registers, logbooks of some kind, but perhaps they are anthologies, textbooks, dissertations, masterpieces. I cannot count them because the pile is so jumbled, but there must be around thirty books there. Looking at them for a long time makes me uneasy. Books want something from people, always, even when they are closed. I know those books out there in the water have titles, and I know the pages are covered with millions of symbols that I could read, but I cannot reach them. They are thick books, they must contain an infinite number of words that want to say something, to explain something, that express the thoughts of the people who wrote them. At first there is no identifiable sound other than the flowing water, but then, beneath the gentle rushing, I hear a furious murmur that grows ever more insistent, like a choir singing through clenched teeth, an atonal, malevolent buzzing that reveals no meaning at all, the stifling lament of ink and paper, the sound books make when they know they are being burned or drowned, the keening of words that will never be read again.

POSEIDON VII

In Lindau, a small town across the lake from the site of the infanticide that I told you about, there is a statue of you, the one I mentioned before. I do not know if this is because the lake there is so large and deep that it seems like a sea, or if you also reign over fresh water. Who can say? You stand there, in the middle of the market square, a scene you would recognise. Fish from the lake, cheese from the mountains, fruit, crusty loaves—in that respect, nothing has changed since the days when you were still worshipped. Your statue is young, slender, you are evidently still limber, even though you have already lived for an infinite length of time, and you always stand there in the same pose, half-leaning on the trident that your brother Zeus once gave you so that you could fight against your father. You see that we still know these things about you, and that too is a form of immortality. No-one in the future will know anything about us. But what I should like to know is, can you remember everything yourself? Your father being so terrified that one of you would murder him that he ate you all? I once saw a painting of that day: your father is truly a monster, clutching one of his children in both hands as if it were a rabbit, his eyes are wide open, his hair is blowing around as if in a storm. In my imagination I could hear the sound of his jaws as he crushes you all. It is a miracle that he spewed you up again whole after your brother put poison in his honey. Is that why you prefer to stay beneath the waves? To avoid your dreadful family? We think we know how the world came into being, an equally violent fairy tale, but without gods, and, for a time, without people. For you gods, everything begins with chaos, while for us it starts with an inconceivably saturated moment of intolerable tension and only then comes the chaos, which continues even today and which we think is order, an ever-expanding mechanical formula. At that moment, time was created, but some of us believe in a god who was always there and will always remain, so that is of course impossible, unless we wish to believe that time did not become an aspect of eternity until the world came into being.

The god I am talking about is, according to those who still believe in Him, eternal and omnipresent. *Altijd*, the Dutch word for "always," is literally "all time," and all of time is eternity, unless eternity has no need of the time before or after the world. All of time: that is the time of the universe, in Dutch the *heelal*, the whole-all in which we live. Whole-all, all-time. But what is it like for you Olympians? You may be gods, but you are eternal only in one direction, as it were, going forwards. The fact is that you have not always been there. The god I am talking about, on the other hand, was always there. Never born; that is the difference. You, though, were born, even your mother was born and, before that, her mother, a child of Day and Air, and kin to dark Night and the impene-trable Underworld. So, you are all part of the same family, and your story vanishes into a cloud of nameless eternity. You have the mists of Chaos as an ancestor, but we cannot erect statues to Chaos. We can build them for you, however, and so I see you here every Saturday when I visit the market. The Cyclopes forged that trident for you, the attribute by which you shall always be recognised. It is a weapon and can be used to kill. I do not know if you can hear me, but perhaps recognition is a kind of worship. In any case, it will have to suffice, even though I know how quick you are to anger.

WALL

Some forms of writing are not intended as such. These unintentional missives can be found on beaches, in the asphalt of a city street, in a newly cut tree trunk, in stone. Communications written in ciphers, messages, codes. Words, graffiti written by no-one. On the island where I live, there is a sandy track that passes through a scorched landscape. Thistles and oak apples, powdery brown dust that forms clouds around your feet as you walk. This is the north, the sea wind has free rein here, as you can see from the trees and the bushes, which have bowed before the violence, becoming grotesque sculptures, their backs turned against the sound of the sea. At the end of the track is a pebble beach, desiccated, brown seaweed, sometimes tinged with the sheen of sea salt. Beside the track, two or three houses, uninhabited. One of them is on a slope, and I climb up there in spite of the heat. The empty circle of a threshing floor with broken, faded red tiles and withered weeds. A cactus like a collapsed Brancusi. The house itself is low, the roof tiles covered with the ochre growth of lichen, the windows broken. An old cart in what was once the stable, its wooden shaft lying alongside. A broken gutter, lead the colour of slate. Shards of glass that glint in the fierce sunlight. On a wall, four bottles, dirty and filled with sand. The silence weighs a ton. I stand before the writing on the wall: scratches in the peeling plaster, flakes of white that look like tainted snow. Tracks, circles, slender furrows—what kind of letters are these? If I stand there long enough, I can read a poem of decay and disintegration, of human absence. A poem in the form of a wall. The north wind, the August heat, the February rains have all helped to write it. When I leave, no-one will read a word in this place.

BLUR

An image has remained with me, even though I did not actually see it. Strange for a film, but that is how it is. It was only said, not shown. There was something to see, but we did not see it: just a white blur, as the person who mentioned it was unable to see clearly at that moment. She had taken off her glasses because she was crying, and then she had rubbed her eyes. The man who has just spoken to her with such hatred, blazing hot and yet ice-cold, is standing a few feet away. We, however, are able to see his face. It is white, all boundless despair and self-pity. As she is not wearing her glasses, she cannot see his face, just that white and blurry patch. She tells him so. The film has made her ugly, a country schoolteacher, but right now she is beautiful. It is great art to show love simply by making a woman in an empty classroom lift her head a little higher to catch a different light. He spoke for a long time, almost in a monotone, with the chill fire of absolute contempt. A litany of measured hate. She loves him and he does not want her. They are together but he is disgusted by her, by her presence, her voice, her tears. Everything he says is an invocation of destruction, but even his hatred is hollow, as is his entire existence, and she knows it. She sees a white blur, a man already almost completely erased, layering on his impotent revulsion, as love is making her more and more beautiful. The final scene is a church service with three people receiving Holy Communion: the lecherous organist looking at his watch, the lame sexton who has been reflecting upon Christ's loneliness in Gethsemane, and the woman, with her love and her big shoes, in that awful sealskin coat. The man she adores looks out into the empty church and begins the service with the same words as ever. The sound of the organ, the strange charm of the Swedish, in which I sometimes hear an echo of my own language, a reminder of archaic times. An empty church in an endless landscape, 1963, the early dusk of the northern winter, no solution, no mercy, life as its own punishment.

POSEIDON VIII

The more I know, the less I know. And there begins the con-fusion. What in Greek, in Hesiod, is called chaos, the chaos from which everything supposedly emerged, your version of "In the beginning God created the heaven and the earth," is, in the most recent English translation of the *Theogony* that I read, simply called "Chasm," an abyss, a hole, something that is wide open, something that is entirely different from chaos. Chaos is all manner of things mixed up together, while an opening is in fact nothing, emptiness, a gap. So, in that sense, you are a great-grandson of nothing. In our tradition, in the beginning, God created something out of nothing. As an eternal being, he already existed, and so he precedes what he makes. You see it differently, however, in a way that is in fact even more mysterious. Those of us who do not believe in God talk about the Big Bang, but what exactly was it that went bang? The mystery of what was there before still remains. I cannot solve it, and perhaps you cannot either, and Hesiod does not explain—why should he? He has his hands full with the intricacies of the hundreds of branches and twigs of your family tree, which is further complicated by the fact that you gods are so like us. Lustful, jealous, copulating, magnificent, warring people who just happen to be immortal and whose stories have captivated the world. Our God had to devise a Son for himself in order to get closer to us but, as Pascal already knew, the puzzle of what He or She or It actually is or was, is too vast for our limited imaginations. The twelfth-century theologian Alain de Lille once came up with the theory that God was a sphere whose centre is everywhere, while its circumference is nowhere, a mysterious mathematical representation that was so appealing that it was later repeated in all kinds of different places, including the works of Rabelais. God as a sphere had already appeared in your own Xenophanes and Parmenides, but no-one has ever told us if you, with your human and divine body, were aware of such speculation. You certainly never mentioned it, so it remains a mystery, and perhaps it is better that way. We are too imperfect a creation to deal with such a vast abstraction, our questions are inadequate for the answers they might receive. We should never have let you go. You brought us closer to storms, love, water, death, wind, fire, the things that make us suffer and live, things we understand. We don't understand anything about that other one. And yet we are supposed to kneel down before that nothing—but who would kneel down before Nothing?

HÖLDERLIN

A postcard from a friend. A picture of a man with his head bowed, and what could be a smile on his face. Looks like a pencil sketch. A few indications of the paper's texture: lighter strands, small spots, fibres. The man's right hand is not visible, he appears to have something in his left. Minimal lines to indicate the seams of his clothing: a crease, the collar, perhaps part of a neckerchief. Everything is light, except for the hair, which seems to be drawn with a thicker pencil. The head is bowed in thought, as if the man has paused and is standing very still in the middle of a room. I think of Goethe and of Schiller, who did not know quite what to make of this timid, yet passionate stranger. In very fine handwritten letters, it says, "Von Schreiner und Rudolph in Eile gezeichnet am 27sten Jul. 23." But why were Schreiner and Rudolph in a hurry if the man they were drawing was standing so still? His eyes are looking at something on the ground, but he appears to be gazing inside and seeing something there that he cannot solve. He does not look like Hölderlin. Nonsense—of course he looks like the Hölderlin that his two friends saw that day. He simply does not resemble the person that I believe Hölderlin to have been. "Die Tage gehn vorbei mit sanfter Lüfte Rauschen," my friend has written beside it in pencil. The days pass with the sound of gentle breezes. Why do I read that line differently now than I did before I saw the drawing?

VEILS

I am not a real diver, but I love to hang beneath that transparent, moving ceiling like some clumsy, extinct marine animal. No-one finds me appetising, so there is no danger. Suspended over the sea floor, I gaze up through my primitive diving goggles at the shifting silver of the surface that looks so different from below than from above, where the same thin membrane seems like a wine-dark curtain rippling back and forth. This is the domain of silence, and everything is possible here. Words still exist, but are stripped of their sound, ghosts consisting solely of language. I see fish that are not startled by me, but what fascinates me most are the veils, the brideless veils swept this way and that by the tide, green, greyish, finely branched. Seaweed, algae, dentate, lobate, silver, vermilion, maiden's hair, cobwebs, intimate, seductive feathers, magic threads. Sometimes their names are reminders of the god to whom I am writing, *Posidonia oceanica*, or of fragments of hymns that are sung to him, *Bryopsis plumosa*, *Caulerpa prolifera*, *Ulva lactuca*, names of women one would like to know. There is one thing a diver must never do, and that is to take something from the god's domain up into the world above, where it does not belong. Then the spell is broken, and dream creatures go astray in the wrong dimension, the one where we belong. And the diver is left standing on the rocks, forlorn, a marine animal transformed back to human, with a handful of wet plants, bizarre forms with no magic, metamorphosis failed.

PAINTING

Berlin, December 30, 1936. A tall, thin man, still young, gazes intently at a painting by Peter Paul Rubens in the Kaiser Friedrich Museum. He does not actually like Rubens, but this painting has captured his attention. He notes that it depicts Neptune and Amphitrite "with fabulous beasts, crocodile, lion, tiger, rhinoceros etc." This painting vanished as booty in the war that was already hanging ominously in the Berlin air, and all that remains is a reproduction in black and white. He explores every inch of the image. The god is sitting, his right leg loosely crossed over the left, one foot in the water. The crocodile close to that foot does not alarm him and neither do the lion and tiger, which are growling at each other, maws wide open, dangerous, or the water nymph draping her voluptuous Flemish body so seductively over the crocodile. The god is in love. His long white beard flows over his chest, the focus of his gaze is unmistakable, his expression is melancholy and full of longing. His left shoulder almost touches the right breast of the goddess, who is not looking at him. This is a peculiar gathering. In the background, one man hugs another, who is pouring water from a gigantic nautilus shell. The goddess is resting her hand on a giant clam, inside which a smaller pearly nautilus nestles against a *Cypraea* and other shells, attributes of the sea god. She is enjoying something but we do not know what, her lips slightly parted, her eyes open but seeing nothing. The upper part of his trident must be somewhere outside the painting, Rubens knew that viewers would complete the image with their own inner gaze. The young man knew that too, and later made increasing use of omission as the most essential feature of his art, his last book, only ten pages long, describing his own demise as he lives through it.

He has been in Berlin for weeks. He eats frugally and sleeps in simple guesthouses, a man alone on a mission. His letters from that period show that he has mastered German. He can read Nazi newspapers, the flags with swastikas are part of the cityscape. He sees everything and stores it in his memory. He walks for miles across the ice-cold city, working his way through museum after museum with methodical precision, and every day he writes his notes, brief descriptions, evaluations. His favourite is Adriaen Brouwer: a bleak landscape, three men absorbed in a game of bowls, a scattering of houses at dusk, a wild patch of light in a dark sky. Future commentators will say that Caravaggio's tenebrism and Rembrandt's chiaroscuro were echoed in his stage sets. Forty years later, he will direct his play *Waiting for Godot* in that same city, but he will not see the painting of the sea god again.

POSEIDON IX

What are names? A name designates a thing or a human being, but that person or object is not actually that name. We bear our names, but we are not them. We depart from our bodies and do not take those names with us, they remain behind as empty shells or as words on a gravestone. Or perhaps it is the other way around and, when our body dies, what we believed ourselves to be cannot endure without that body and so vanishes into the same state of absence as before our birth.

I mention this because I wanted to know where your name comes from. Cicero does not wish to get his fingers burned and, in an endless and cunning dialogue about the gods, he sits on the fence, but still reveals through a number of sarcastic remarks that he has problems with you deities, the power you have over us, your origins and also your names. Then he forgets that you are of Greek stock and gently mocks your Latin name: "though"—says the made-up Carneades to the equally fictitious Balbus—"since you think the name Neptune comes from *nare*, 'to swim,' there will be no name of which you could not make the derivation clear by altering one letter: in this matter you seem to me to be more at sea than Neptune himself!" Shortly before, the same book mentions the gods who are gods even though they were born of mortal mothers, and there he asks if your son Theseus and "all the other sons of gods" should "also be reckoned as gods."

You must admit that it is strange for life and death to commingle, but that is what happens when you father a child with someone who must one day die. It is like some elevated form of marrying beneath your station, but with fatal consequences for your child.

Had Cicero read Plato's *Cratylus*, the dialogue on the same subject? The usual procedure: Socrates, who already knows everything, leads his interlocutor a merry dance until the poor man is worn out and humbly concedes that Socrates is right about everything. My Greek is now so rusty that I hardly dare comment, yet still I feel that a travesty of etymology has occurred, in which every sudden brainwave is seen as equally valid. Poor Cratylus, who is defeated in the dialogue, believes that some divine power doles out names, and, for that reason alone, names must be right. He has set a trap for himself, though, because the jesuitical Socrates goes on to ask him, "Then, in your opinion, he who gave the names, though he was a spirit or a god, would have given names which made him contradict himself?" Cratylus attempts to wriggle out of it by saying that some words are not actually names, but the next trap is already waiting and the conversation simmers on in that vein until Socrates cries out, "Stop for Heaven's sake! Did we not more than once agree that names which are rightly given are like the things named and are images of them?" For "things" here, one may also read people, because he has previously ensnared Cratylus by asking if Cratylus and the image of Cratylus are two different things. Cratylus opts for himself in duplicate, but he is still not out of the woods. It is only after almost two hundred densely printed pages that Socrates finally allows him to leave for the countryside, presumably to recover from his dizziness. Your name has come up in the meantime, as Socrates thinks out loud about how it was given to you by the person who first used it, when the strength of the sea made it hard for him to walk, as if you had put a sort of shackle (*desmos*) around his feet (*podōn*). He arrives at your name via *posidesmon*, "a foot-bond," and says that the *e* must have been added for the sake of euphony. I try to imagine it. One day, in an unimaginable antiquity, when you were not yet called Poseidon, a man is walking along a beach somewhere. Now and then he paddles in the water, up to his ankles, just as I like to do, feeling the force of the sea resisting his feet, and he imagines a name for you, a story like a short poem. But perhaps that is not correct, says Socrates, promptly upsetting his own applecart, and then he comes up with something even more complicated in an attempt to explain your byname of Earth-Shaker.

As you never answer me, I shall never find out what you think about all of this, but when I stare out at the grey, slowly shifting North Sea from the beach at IJmuiden, as I did yesterday, I think of you quietly rocking out there in your waves and most probably devoting no thought to the subject at all, and that takes me back to the beginning: what, in the end, is a name?

ORION

At around midnight, here in a Germanic winter on the edge of the Alps, I see him again, Orion, the blind hunter, the moon man of the mountains, Poseidon's son, the most beautiful man there ever was, lured into bed by insatiable Eos, the dawn, who was tormented by unflagging lust as a punishment when Aphrodite caught her in bed with Ares, the god of war. I know Orion from winter nights in Amsterdam, when I see his shape above one of the canals. Then he is a man of winter, high and cold, always on the move with his hounds, but in the month of August, I meet him again on my Spanish island, where he appears at the end of the night, just after the Pleiades have appeared above the horizon, and flees in the light of the dawn that once seduced him. Women were his undoing. He is the brightest, yet the saddest of all the constellations, and perhaps that is why I love him. On Chios he fell for Merope, granddaughter of Dionysus, daughter of King Oenopion. He would be allowed to marry her once he had freed the island from wild animals. This is a story of deceit, for after Orion has accomplished his task, Oenopion does not keep his side of the bargain. One drunken night, Orion takes Merope by force, whereupon Oenopion puts out Orion's eyes. Orion, now blind, rows to Lemnos, where he finds an apprentice at the forge of Hephaestus, who will carry him on his shoulders halfway around the world to the ends of the ocean, where Eos falls in love with him, and her brother, the Sun, returns his eyesight. Orion now wants to take revenge on Oenopion, but on his quest he meets Artemis, who, like him, is obsessed with the hunt.

They hunt together, but Apollo interferes by sending a monstrous scorpion to pursue Orion. He can do nothing to defeat that hideous creature's armour. Orion flees into the sea, his father's ocean, but what is a mortal to do when the gods are against him? Apollo tells Artemis that the swimmer in the sea is someone else, a man who has seduced one of her priestesses. The goddess aims for the head of the distant swimmer and kills him, but when she swims over to the body she sees that it is Orion. She asks Asclepius, Apollo's son, to bring him back to life, but as he is about to do so Zeus hurls a thunderbolt and kills Asclepius before he can accomplish his task. Artemis places Orion's ever-familiar image among the other stars, where he is still pursued every night by the Scorpion, and that is how I see him now in the cold, clear sky: a man who was too handsome to live, the target of women's lust, forever out hunting with Sirius, his dog, the twinkling star at his feet. I know the names of all his stars, and that one of his shoulders, Betelgeuse, is infinitely stronger than the sun, I know how far apart the stars of his sword and his belt are, and that, one day, unimaginable millennia from now, the laws of the universe will cause them to move so far apart that nothing of him will remain, a lost hunter, torn asunder by time, but this does not detract from his enchantment, the image and the story are too strong, even now. He is my patron saint, the most recognisable constellation. I am always pleased to see him, a mortal who was loved by goddesses, and who had the gods against him.

PASTORALE

Now that the snow has gone, the birds arrive. The trees outside the window are bare, their bark flaking and scabrous, covered with moss, which seems to offer sufficient nourishment for the great tits. Brown leaves and broken branches lie out on the field, which has suddenly reverted to green. In the distance, patches of snow, clouds of mist. A jay comes in a flash of colour, first takes a look, hops about a little, then starts pecking at the ground, there are no acorns now, just small, invisible things, apparently not worms. The jay is doing what people refer to as work, providing for itself. It is as if we were to get up in the morning and go searching nearby for our food in a rather complicated manner, and to remain occupied with that task from morning to night. I do not know why the jay chooses this spot and then, after a while, abruptly flies away, having investigated only a few square metres of the large meadow, when there is still so much more. Was it just an appetiser? Is the main course elsewhere? One thing is clear, what for me is a view, pasture, trees, distant mountains, is food for the great tit and the jay. Jay makes a meal for the fox; great tit is a dish for owl and buzzard. Nature is edible. Dinner is served.

POSEIDON X

The British queen's art collection includes a drawing of you by Leonardo da Vinci, in which you look furious. I cannot quite tell from the reproduction, but I think it is a pencil drawing. It appears to have been done quickly, perhaps so as to capture your rage. Tangled pencil lines curl together, converging with the wild sea foam and the tails and manes of the team of animals that pulls your chariot so swiftly across the ocean. Your arm with the trident is raised high in the air, but the movement is a downward one, as if you wish to use those sharp points to fire up the already wild horses. You are furious with Odysseus for plucking out the eye of one of your offspring when he had only the one; such an act is unforgivable. The unfortunate Polyphemus had asked the name of the man who had done this to him and Odysseus made him an eternal laughing stock by answering that his name was Nobody. Beneath the belly of a sheep, he had escaped the cave of the Cyclops that had killed his friends. Nobody escapes the vengeance of the gods, but if that nobody is called Odysseus, then you will pursue him for years, hunt him down, take him prisoner, attempt to drown him, until Athene, the daughter of your brother

Zeus, comes to the assistance of the ever-fugitive hero, and he may finally return home, first to Ithaca, and subsequently to the eternal pages of the world's treasury of tales, where his story will be told again and again into infinity. But this time it is not about you, but about your horses. Seahorses are known to be very small creatures, certainly too small to transport a god, and yet story has it that your golden sea chariot was pulled by four giant hippocampi. In myths and legends, big and small have no meaning, and reality can be shrunk or expanded at will, this is the fabulator's privilege. But if you were that close to your seahorses, did you discover their secrets too? Did you know the seahorse is the only species in which the males become pregnant? Have you ever observed seahorses in the calm depths of your endless oceans, courting in that mysterious vertical position by hooking together the last curl of their incredibly flexible tails and dancing? Aristotle came close to their secret, he may have known that the minuscule miraculous creature with that strange, equine head was a fish with gills. He knew the mysteries of the related pipefish, but he could not look beneath the water and see the moment of conception, as two seahorses turn their graceful heads to face each other, lips and bellies touching to form a heart, and the female conjures up a sort of tube from within herself and slides it into an opening in the male's abdomen, all without letting go of him. They lift up those elegant horseheads, their backs are curved—this is a moment of great excitement. After a courtship that may have lasted for days, the mating is over in six or seven seconds, the female squirting her egg-saturated fluid into him, and as soon as he is full, the pregnant male lets his festive courtship attire fade, like a chameleon, and steals away. He wriggles and jiggles for a while until the eggs are where they should be, in a sort of inner hatchery, and three weeks later he will experience something that males of no other species on earth know: the pain of giving birth.

Do gods read philosophers? Do you know your Seneca, his *De ira*? No matter how furious you were with Odysseus, I cannot imagine that you would have threatened your four seahorses with your trident as you do in that drawing by Leonardo. As for myself, I can no longer sit in the early morning on the island on a rock by the sea, as I have done so often before, without thinking about the ritual choreography that might at that very moment be taking place in the unseen depths.

CONVERSATION

The emperor asks the prince what sort of woman the author is. A monstrous schemer, replies the prince, I owe my position here to her, and that is proof enough. So she is a good friend, says the emperor. She? A friend? She is capable of throwing her friends into the river so that she can pull them back out again on a fishhook. One must have had the good fortune of having slept with her to know what it is to love an animal. The emperor says nothing more.

A few years later, when the emperor is no longer an emperor but the prince is still a prince, the prince receives news of her death, and he completes her portrait: "Capricious in her hatred as in her friendships, in her tastes as in her anger, there was much of the pampered old coquette about her."

AGAVE

He stood in my Spanish garden for forty years, he was already there when I first came. He never said hello, never asked any questions. I gave him water in the summer months, but he made it clear that he hardly required any. He stores water in his leaves, where it becomes poisonous— for us, not for the plant. My plant book describes him as a succulent with large, powerful, basal rosettes, but he would probably find that kind of language too romantic. His leaves are elongated, narrower between the base and the middle, thick and fleshy, with a spiny edge and a vicious tip. I am sure the plant himself would never phrase it that way, though. The trees I had planted around him, and those, like the oleasters, which had arrived of their own accord, were starting to deprive him of light. He had decided to pay them no heed. He had his own task to perform. I realised that if he had been able or willing to speak, he would probably have done so with a Mexican accent. I loved that plant. I say this in the past tense, because my plant is doomed to die. I find his approaching death so bewildering that I wander between tenses, and it makes me a little dizzy. He is still standing there, and yet he is dying, but he is acting as if nothing were wrong, and I am finding that hard to deal with; after all, I have known him for forty years. Around him, a network of offspring has grown rampant, a bunch of clones with tangled daggers, taking up residence beneath him, and causing him to grow askew. As a result, more and more of his roots have pushed up above the ground, a swelling covered with a web of dry brown threads. His leaves are two colours, sea green with a pale sort of yellow around the edges, trimmed with those mean points; I always had to be on my guard. Every year, when I returned, the bottom leaves had turned brown and withered, like the leather bindings of decaying books in a dark cellar, secrets that could no longer be deciphered. Where I had cut them back, bitter wounds remained, bearing witness to his age. He tolerated his skewed stance with angry dignity, the innermost circle of his leaves thrusting unsheathed swords up into the light. He saw me growing older all those years, but I do not know what he thought about time and duration, or if he even wanted to measure them. Maybe he knew he was his own measure, and his own purpose. This year he arrived at the point where he needed to be. Suddenly, among those dangerous leaves in the middle of his rosette, a supple green stalk appeared, becoming taller by the day. The speed was frightening, it grew a decimetre every twenty-four hours, a green phallus raised aloft in search of consummation, bending with the breeze. When it could grow no more, clusters appeared at the top and swelled, becoming fuller and fuller, yellow-green buds reaching up high, each elongated bullet the promise of a female flower. And then my agave would die, mission accomplished. A direct line led from him to the Big Bang; there is no such thing as coincidence, as he had always known. For me, all that will soon remain is the empty spot beneath the palm and the oleaster. Perhaps one of his underlings would like to start over again. He sows uncertainty about his identity. *Agave marginata*, the book says. And also: hundred-year aloe. But then it adds in a whisper: "in spite of what the name suggests, this plant is not an aloe." It would not surprise me at all if he were secretly a writer.

POSEIDON XI

All-seeing. Omnipresent. This was said about our God. The comparison with you continues to suggest itself, even though you might find that annoying. The possibility of seeing everything, of being everywhere at the same time, but in your case I limit that to the sea, even though I know better. And I know better because in the *Iliad* alone you become involved in a land battle, and later you get up to all kinds of tricks with the sea to thwart Odysseus, while according to Kafka you generally remain beneath the waves. So Kafka's image has won out over Homer, and that is why it will not let me go. I read that Borges, when he was leaving Buenos Aires for a long period on a ship sailing slowly out of the mouth of the River Plate, once threw a coin into the water from the top deck, perhaps as people do at the Trevi Fountain in Rome, in the hope that one day they may return.

As I read that story, I pictured the coin finding its way into the depths. I imagined the coin, so deep down, being corroded by seawater and slowly, maybe over the course of centuries, perishing, and in that image I saw a metaphor for the work of the poet, sinking equally slowly into the depths of time, until no-one knew whose words they were, or what they meant, a thought that would have been recognised by Borges, who once said that one person's entire oeuvre might remain, while for another it might be a poem and for yet another just a sentence or a few words that have ensconced themselves within the language, minus the poet's name, without anyone remembering where they came from.

You, who are everywhere and notice everything, would of course have seen that coin sinking. Once I had pictured it, it seized hold of me. How many things have you seen floating down into the depths? And how quickly does it happen? Can you measure it? The doge's ring, once a year in Venice's golden days, just a small, glittering object thrown from the deck of the *bucintoro*, a wedding ring that you received, year after year, as the city, where there are so many statues of you, also married your sea, year after year. I imagine the ring sank very slowly into the brown water of the lagoon, but how do other objects fare?

How slowly does a person sink? And what does it look like? Do the fish and other hunters chase after a corpse as it tumbles and twirls into the deep from a great height and then floats back up again? Is it crushed, pulverised under the pressure that you bear with such ease? Sailors, pirates, divers, shark victims, shipwrecks, suicides? How long does a metallic object take to travel six thousand metres through the endless, sunless halls of your depths? Did that Air France plane with those hundreds of people on board sail down slowly or quickly? Did it let the currents lead it in some kind of slow-motion dance? An emotionless robot located the wreckage with the dead still inside, like, before them, the *Titanic*, the *Graf Spee*, and those sailors in the Russian submarine, the *Kursk*, who died so slowly. Perhaps you do not wish to explain what it looks like; it must be a kind of dreadfully silent ballet, one that you have seen all too often, the slowest dance without music.

WALK

From my window, first the meadow, then the ranks of tall pines, black warriors, deathly still. They are waiting for the enemy to attack. Above the army, the hill, some farmhouses, a second wood lying on the slope like a large, lazy animal. When I go downstairs and leave the house, I become that romantic phenomenon, the solitary walker, an essential component of those dark paintings of the late nineteenth century. What is the solitary walker thinking about? We do not know and we are not supposed to, as that would make him less solitary, which is no good for the painting. I am now walking past the last patch of snow of recent weeks, nearly everything has melted, leaving behind filthy mud that sucks at my shoes with a slurping sound. After the white of the snow, the earth is now deep black, and, where the ground is still slightly frozen, I struggle to keep my balance. I follow the tracks of the gamekeeper's tractor, high ridges, gleaming wet, with a few grey remnants of frozen snow lying between. I continue along the path towards the stream. The water is high because of all the melting snow, I can hear it talking, the privilege of the solitary walker, as is the hunting cry of the buzzard. That high-pitched ee-hee-hee is meant for me, I know that. Where the tractor's trail turns left, there is a primitive wooden rack with hay for the deer. Over the past few weeks I have seen the tracks they left walking to the rack and to the brook; those are gone now, but sometimes, towards evening, I see the deer themselves, soft shadows, briefly visible at the edge of the forest. The forest is black—no, that is not right, all kinds of things are hidden within that blackness—but everything around me is black, until the path takes a turn and the light strikes me. The hills I can see from my window begin here, at the bridge, but I do not walk on yet. I lean over the iron railing and look at the rapid water, the play of light on the transparent, swirling ripples, the brown and grey stones beneath. I never see any fish, even though the stream is quite wide. At this point, another painter takes over; that must be so, because as I walk towards the sun, fire blazes in the windows of the farmhouse at the top of the hill. With every stroke of his brush, I become someone else.

WITNESS

Is a person who has been dead for a few thousand years as dead as someone who died last year? Is there a hierarchy in the kingdom of the dead, giving those with more experience of death a different status from the newcomers, those who have not yet been touched by eternity, but who still smell of time, of life? Are there social distinctions between mummies and corpses?

These are questions that occurred to me as I was looking at a photograph taken at the Egyptian Museum in Cairo, recently visited by looters. They had turned the place upside down, looking not for mummies, but for gold and jewels. Sarcophagi lay topsy-turvy, and somewhere on the floor was a dead man's head. A face that looked like it had once been accustomed to giving orders. I do not know who or what he was. A nobleman, an administrator, a priest, a lawyer? Mummies have no lips, and so their teeth appear larger than those of living people. This dead man's teeth were remarkably intact. One might have thought he was smiling, had the rest of his face not been so stiff and serious. It was a distinguished face—not just anyone was embalmed and wrapped in bandages before departing on that eternal journey. Stiff is perhaps not the right word, though. Outraged would be better, or perhaps bewildered. Who had so rudely awakened him after a few thousand years of sleep? The head wanted to know why it was lying on the floor in such an undignified manner, and without the rest of the body that had always accompanied it, in a room that looked nothing like the place where it had lain in the darkness for all those centuries. That had been the first change to which it could not become accustomed, the sudden light, the voices in impossible languages. You get used to being dead, especially when you have been doing it for thousands of years. Ever since he had been taken from his own familiar tomb and brought to this room, light had been a constant torment, relieved only once a day. But the next morning it was back again, white and cold, as if the very sun, which he could no longer see for himself, were frozen and could produce only this stark whiteness. And with that light came the voices, but eventually he had grown used to them too, until that day when the cries of insurrection had found their way inside. It had been the sound of the masses, of revolt. What he realised then was that he had once more become part of time, and that, with those grasping hands that had pulled off his wrappings in search of hidden treasure, slow eternity had also been torn away from him, and he was once again taking part in something as inconceivable as an event, and therefore in life.

POSEIDON XII

Ovid, Homer, you crop up everywhere, you involved yourself in the big stories, and yet in the real world you remained invisible; there will be those who say that was your downfall. You tormented Odysseus on his way to Ithaca and, together with Athene, you helped Achilles against Apollo on the banks of the raging Scamander, but how much did you love the Greeks of later centuries, people who continued to worship you, but who did not end up in a literary masterpiece? Where were you in 338 B.C. when Philip II of Macedon defeated the Athenians and the Thebans at Chaeronea, heralding the end of their civilisation? Is that part of being a god, manifesting yourselves exclusively in forms of fiction, and making yourselves scarce when it matters? Were all of those prayers and sacrifices in vain? Chaeronea in Boeotia, you should have been there. I read about it in Polybius' history of the world, but it feels like reading today's newspaper, troop movements, envoys, alliances, deception, battles. It has never ceased and it continues into my own era: Syria, Egypt, Libya. Polybius could have carried on writing, because even now no god is concerned about it. Demosthenes accused the Arcadians of being traitors to Greece for fighting alongside Philip the Macedonian. How long does the memory of betrayal last? More than two thousand years have passed and the impoverished Greece of now does not wish the independent Macedonia of now to bear the name of once upon a time, because Greece itself still contains a piece of that quondam country within its own borders. Polybius makes a clear judgement about the reproach of Demosthenes. "For it was by their bringing Philip into the Peloponnese, and humbling the Lacedaemonians, that these men in the first place enabled all its inhabitants to breathe again, and conceive the idea of liberty," he says. Sounds of mourning for this lost greatness would not be heard until later, until Cavafy, whose mirror game of anachronisms predicted the rise of the barbarians and the downfall of Hellenism, a future disguised as the past. You did not wish to prevent that downfall. Or were you unable to, because it no longer involved a myth, but reality, history, facts? Those who have the power may bring along their own gods, while those who lose power must abandon theirs. If you look at it that way, the temples still standing to you are evidence of your impotence. Empty marble husks, with the wind blowing through them. It is only in stories that you were able to survive, but which god will appear when the barbarians come?

CHAIR

The flight from Seoul to Tokyo is delayed by four hours; no succinct description exists for the kind of time following such an announcement. Buses and taxis pull up onto the wide pavement in front of the airport and drive away again. Beyond that, a demolition site, cranes, concrete, the disorderly landscape that belongs with airports in some countries. In the distance I can see some green, but it is not easy to get to. All around, men with yellow helmets are working with cables and wires that lead to an underground world. I have to pass through all kinds of fresh trenches, past ramparts of cement, and then I am there. It is a hillock, a remnant of what might once have been a park. As I walk up through the wild grass, which no-one cuts anymore, small silvery insects fly out ahead of me.

The sound of bulldozers and heavy trucks comes from every direction, the military music of progress. Broken branches; a typhoon narrowly missed Korea yesterday. Then some oriental conifers, like a Chinese or Japanese drawing, ink with water, everything slightly erased, wiped away, almost the bush itself, but never entirely. Then I see it, like a revelation whose significance I cannot yet comprehend: an incredibly blue plastic chair standing beneath a few pine trees, a scream in an empty room. I approach it cautiously, as if there were a risk of danger. The branches of the trees above the chair hang down to form a screen that grows unevenly, touching the ground at only one end. Whoever put this chair here knew what he was doing. Someone must use it often, a few cigarette ends are scattered around it as a message: this is not your chair. And I know that. I am the intruder here. Now I notice that there are very thin silver and gold threads around the tree trunks, tied with a minimal bow, magical missives to the spirit of the trees. The person who belongs to the chair has locked his bicycle to one of the trunks. I stand there for a moment, very still, and then I sit. From this position, the other man must see every day what I see now: dry soil covered with needles and small pinecones, a piece of sawn wood, some scorched grass. A cricket spins its prayer wheel, quietly, as though embarrassed or surprised by the loneliness of that sound. There is nothing else, a light breeze, the rustling of branches, a magpie with a blue sheen to its wings, like the flag of some unknown country. Further away, back where I came from, the noise and the movement of the world. Aeroplanes, excavators, the rancid architecture of an airport. Now I can feel the moment stretching out, I might have been sitting here for a hundred years, a man on a blue throne beneath a baldachin of pine branches, a plastic king with no subjects.

When that century has passed, I renounce my throne and walk slowly and ceremoniously down the hillock and through the dying park. No, I do not walk. I stride. As I reach the border, I turn around one more time to say fare-well. There it stands, so quiet and still, the bluest chair in the whole world. The secret of some friendships is impossible to explain to other people.

DONKEYS

There is sound, and there is light. The sound is of hoofs on stone, but I cannot yet see where it is coming from. The light is southern, Mediterranean. It shines from above, through high windows, lighting up walls the colour of very pale sand. No decoration, no other colours.

What I see is an empty room, the very earliest Gothic, a deliberate impression of Cistercian frugality, reinforced by its height. The sound comes from around the corner, the clattering of hoofs. Not horses, smaller than that. Then I see the first of the donkeys. It is a small herd, six, seven grey donkeys, ill at ease in this bare, solemn space.

It is a moment before I realise what is strange about them. Their stance. Their heads are not down, they are not grazing. Stone is inedible. I have a donkey as a neighbour in Spain, and he has a whole field of grass to devour. That is his job: to eat the field bare. He wakes in the morning, surrounded by his food, and he begins. I have never known him to do anything else. When the winter is over, he can start all over again; he will strip the field until he drops down dead, a Sisyphean end. The donkeys here have no such task. When they stop moving for a moment, the silence is unbearable.

One starts walking, and the others follow. The sound of twenty-eight hoofs on the medieval stone is a composition, written, note by note, by an unseen composer: trot, silence, a few steps, and then running until they become breathless at the sound they produce in these high halls. One of the donkeys needs to pee. Bracing its hind legs, it stands there very tensely, and the flood sounds like a mountain stream as the others are all standing still. Then the walking begins again, a journey that leads nowhere. I can see them on three screens, the sharp light catching the nuances in their grey coats, their ears up like antennae, the scratching of their small hoofs on the shiny stones, their timid halt, the lack of a goal, the renewed motion. I know this is something devised by humans, that the image and sound were dreamed up for me, that the room I can see is not the room where I am, that I can see them and they cannot see me. When I close my eyes I hear them, an occasional snort, a gust of wind blowing through that space. They do not bray. Somebody wanted a meaning, something metaphorical, and they are presenting it: seven donkeys in the Palace of the Popes in Avignon. The only sense I can make of it is seven silent popes in a stable without hay, all giving shape to the same answerless question with their shod feet.

GARDEN

The temple is ancient, the garden that is not a garden has been here for five hundred years. The rocks are mountains, the bushes distant forests. If you do not believe this, you should not come here. I first visited years ago and every piece of gravel has remained the same. The gravel is water, and I watch it rippling and glinting. In the middle is an island, a female turtle made of stone. No deceit could be more subtle. The smaller island swimming beside the turtle is her child. I look at the raked waves of gravel. They are moving towards the other, larger island, an island called crane. Everything means something different, and everything means itself. A crane is a crane. Anyone who does not see those wings must be mad.

The turtle seeks out the bottom of the ocean, that abyss of evil in which one can drown; the crane wishes to leave this world. Which do you want to be? Pay attention to the ship sailing across the stone waves. Life moves in only one direction. The omniscient water flows into the next garden. Having reconciled turtle and crane, it flows on as a river to the ocean in which life pours, freed from all contradictions, from the battle of existence. A person who sees only stone will see no waterfall, no river, no island, no ocean. Another man once tried it with bread and wine. I sit on the wooden walkway and listen to the sound of the waves. Somewhere down there, a stone Poseidon must dwell, recording fate in a book made of water. The world as illusion.

I cannot remember how long ago I was last here. The time between then and now has evaporated, like a life. The monk at the exit has also grown older. He wants to know where I come from, as he did back then. Signing my book, he quietly sings the "Wilhelmus" for me, the Dutch national anthem. This repetition makes time seem, for a second, like eternity.

POSEIDON XIII

For how long can a person look at a stone? Cézanne gazed for hours at an apple, certain objects make their own demands when you wish to know something about their essence. An apple for an artist, a stone for the poet. It is lying here beside me, on the desk at which I write. You could call it grey, but is that really true? Its shape is an irregular oval, and it must weigh at least a kilo. I found it one day on the beach and lugged it in my basket on a long walk. Since then, it has lain outside in an oven in the garden of my house on the island. You must know it, my island. Odysseus came here, of course, and I know that you always kept track of him, if only to annoy him.

Why am I writing this to you? Because the stone here beside me is the only tangible object of yours that I possess. No date is written at the beginning of myths, so I do not know how old you are, but if I wish to claim that you made this stone, you would need to be at least 350 million years old, because the stone is from the Devonian period, the fourth subdivision of the Palaeozoic era. Now I place my hand on the stone for a moment, because its antiquity lends it an aura of immortality that calls for reverence. So, gently, I rest my hand on the stone. What do I feel? Coolness, and time. I hold it with two hands, lift it slightly and feel its weight. Grey, I said, but the more I look, the more I doubt. It is like all those metres of white in the habits of Zurbarán's monks; when you come closer it is no longer white, but has all kinds of colours shimmering within it, nuances of white and grey and blue and gold. The same is true of my stone. Narrow rivers of white and rust run through it, streams and brooks with many branches. Other parts of the stone have a cloudy sheen of dirty white.

But the strangest thing of all is a broad, yellow-white band that seems to divide my stone in two, and yet when I turn the stone over I see that it does not go all the way around, as if something went wrong during its creation. Yes, of course you made it, once upon a time, when you shook the earth in the Devonian. You are the Earth-Shaker, are you not? And that was not all. You stood there boiling, perhaps jealous of Hephaestus, who is known as Vulcan in that other language for good reason. You mixed and shook great masses of stone, folding them, pleating them into almost female forms in moments of unimaginable heat, and then your walls of rock emerged, a newly made landscape that could be seen by no-one, because there were as yet no humans. What was that like, being a god without people? Is there any point? Were you bored? Anyway, you began, in your other form, as god of the sea, to eat away at your own work of art with salt and with storms, and you have continued to do so ever since. What happens? A chunk of a cliff face breaks off, and another, and another. One of the beaches here on my island is evidence of that. It is difficult to access, a climb through thistles and vicious bushes, but it is worth the effort. You have created something there that is truly strange, a sea of stones that have polished one another over the long centuries. They are round, smooth, veined with other lighter-coloured kinds of stones, slate, sandstone, the iron in them has oxidised to the blood colour of rust. It is impossible to lie on the beach, or to walk normally; it is a case of keeping your balance and leaping across the larger rocks, from stone to stone. Perhaps you saw me. Just another mortal on one of your coasts, a man dancing across your work of art and trying not to fall, bending down to free one stone from among all those others and carrying it home so that he can think about you, about you and the fate of gods and mortals, and then, back in the quiet of his own house, picking up the stone once again, as if holding that petrified coolness were the same as holding time itself in his hands.

GIRL

Late evening in Nagasaki. It was the day I visited Dejima, an island only two hundred metres long, which lies in the bay like a fan made of stone. A few centuries ago, the Netherlanders of the Dutch East India Company lived here, the only westerners who were allowed to set foot in this place, and Japan's only connection with the rest of the world. They were allowed into the city only with the permission of the Japanese authorities, and the rest of Japan was off limits, a peculiar form of captivity. Where once the sea touched the shore, there is now a new district of the city. The old prints reveal a different picture. A rigged seventeenth-century Dutch ship is anchored in the harbour, as ships were not allowed to moor along the shore either. Lighters travelled back and forth between ship and shore, transferring this first multinational's goods, which had come from Amsterdam or Batavia, or from the African ports along the route. The arrival of that one ship was the event of the year on Dejima.

I already knew that space is not time, but in such places it is easy to become confused. *Then* mingles with *there* when I visit the old trading post and look at books containing words in my language as it was back then, long lists of Dutch names. The men who belonged to those names came from my city. They travelled for years or months. Time was a different substance, tough, stretched, like treacle; there was less of it and everything lasted longer. The *then* of those men and ships wraps itself around me. I do not return to the *now* until I reach the Atomic Bomb Museum. There, too, time has something to say, a twisted, offended clock stopped at the moment of the bomb, two minutes past eleven in the morning. On a wooden wall, a shadow that was once a body, a scorched shade. The survivors are eerier than the charred corpses.

Later I walk along the quayside, and the dark hills across the water are the same as in those prints of long ago. The hoarse cry of a late ferry, my own footsteps on the wood of the jetty, the sudden high waves of an unseen ship. Then I hear her. Quiet at first, so I do not know where the sound is coming from. Then louder, and I can find her, she is sitting with her guitar on a stone ledge at the foot of a kind of dyke, her legs dangling above the water. She is alone, her voice sweet and high, a song in her language, echoing around the entire bay. Even when I am much further away, I can still hear her, a woman singing to the sea. The god must surely have heard her too.

BLOOD MOON

Blood moon, hunter's moon—that is the name of the moon tonight. It is the full moon of this October day, keeping its appointment as promised, now a truly heavenly body as it hangs large and round above the horizon facing the setting sun, acting, for long minutes, as if it will never move again. Planet and star—one appears to have painted the other with vermilion to suit the evening mood. I look out over the Mediterranean landscape, soon it will be dusk, and the owl will call out nearby, and the curlews in the distance, by the sea. So far everything is as it should be, I understand this, fig tree, oleasters, nothing is moving, this is me, this is my garden, my island, my world, my universe. In my Spanish newspaper today, an article about the new Nobel Prize winners: Perlmutter, Schmidt, Riess, the masters of the hunt for the supernovas.

The man who wrote the story knows his audience: readers who will finish the piece and then glance uncertainly at the skies to see if everything he says is true, if the universe really is expanding as we watch, even though it seems so still tonight. Perhaps I understand the comparison because the writer uses the word "nuts," part of my own name, as a *nooteboom*, in Dutch, is a nut tree. When you put a nut loaf in the oven, he writes, the dough expands, but the nuts do not. The galaxies are the nuts and the space between them stretches. *Estirar*, to stretch. No matter which galaxy you are in as you look out at the universe, he says, you will always believe that you are standing still, while the rest is moving away from you, more quickly as the distance increases. This speed, however, is a deception, the galactic nuts remain where they are, it is the mass of dough around them that . . . Yes, what exactly does it do? *Que se hincha*, the article says, and the dictionary does its best to help: *hincharse* 1. to swell, swell up; to become distended, bloated (stomach) 2. to stuff oneself with (food) 3. to become conceited, vain 4. to make a pile, to make a mint. Now the writer returns to his previous comparison, the nut loaf. It is a little easier to understand the loaf expanding than the same thing happening to the cosmos. We use Einstein's theory of relativity to understand the latter process, he says. When he says "we," he cannot be referring to me, but I listen anyway. In the meantime, it has become dark in my conceited universe, but I sit here peacefully, a child listening to a story. The loaf grows larger within the space where it is located, but the universe does not. Space and time—the voice now becomes captivating—are an intrinsic part of the universe; they arose simultaneously. I feel as if I am being led by the hand, the teacher taking another step forward and telling me that a supernova is a star that explodes and that the light it gives off as it does so could outshine an entire galaxy. The supernovas that make the most light have a mass as large as the sun's, but before they explode they can be as small as the earth. They are known as SN Ia, and their density is so great that if you were to say: I'd like a litre of future SN Ia, they would have to give you a bottle with a mass of two tonnes.

The curlews begin to call. I know they are close to the sea, but I have not yet seen them. Their Dutch name, *griel*, is a better match than "curlew" for that drawn-out, pleading sound they make. The owl I can hear nearby is another member of the secret service; it wears the darkness like a uniform and makes itself invisible.

I ponder the energy of the void, and how emptiness is not the same as nothing, how the only thing capable of accelerating the expansion of the universe is *energía oscura*, a magical formula in itself, dark energy that is part of the void, what would remain if we could remove all matter and radiation from the cosmos. The fact that emptiness is not the same as nothing corresponds in a perfectly unprovable way to the bats that have started to dart in and out of what little light there is, like elementary particles, on their fluttering, unpredictable paths, but the fact that the same void can exert a gravitational recoil effect on itself, making the universe not only expand but also do so more quickly, does not seem to correspond to anything. I hear the voice go on talking about the energy of the emptiness that makes up 75 per cent of the density of the universe, and how the rest is matter, including the ordinary matter of which we and the stars are made, but by then the moon has already climbed above the oleasters, the red has long since turned to ochre and the ochre to silver, the voice disappears into the distance, there is rustling all around me, the owl has found its first victim, the shriek of the field mouse echoes the pain of one substance transforming into another, and then a light mist rises, draping a veil over every secret.

POSEIDON XIV

No, it was not a dream, it was one of those drowsy states of not waking, not sleeping, when we see things that cannot be real. What I saw was you dancing, but you were not alone. There were three of you, all holding tridents, which made you look like triplets performing some infernal jig. It was only when I looked for longer that I recognised you all, the first by his goat's legs, the second by the dot on his forehead, his long wild hair and the ring of fire around him, and you by your beard, which was swirling furiously. The devil looked as he does in medieval images of the Day of Judgment, when he uses his trident to push the vulnerable naked bodies of the sinners into the fires of hell, his face twisted into a grim smile, his eyes the colour of sulphur; he was dancing ecstatically and leaping high, you could smell the scent of burning. Shiva was there in his manifestation as destroyer, in that strange position with his left leg turned sideways over his right, the demon at his feet, the halo of flames around his head. His trident does not look like yours, the prongs of his weapon curve strangely, too elegantly; they must make nasty wounds that become inflamed and suppurate. As for you, you looked as I have always imagined you in your rage, mouth wide open, whirling your arms around like the sails of a windmill. The ground shook, you jumped up and down with both feet at the same time, they must have felt it all over the earth, somewhere a tidal wave must have swept onto the land and drowned people. I could not hear any music, but there must have been a pandemonium of loud, clashing sounds, the light was brass, you stepped apart and moved together again, at one point your tridents became entangled and briefly it appeared as though you were about to let fly at one another, but it did not come to that. There was a great roar of laughter and you danced away over the horizon. I woke to an ash-coloured morning, which felt strangely appropriate.

MAN

I have no idea why I should think of him in a strange hotel room on the other side of the world—I do not understand the workings of my own mind. But suddenly, there he was, the man in his chair, the man in front of his house, the man on the pavement. I call him the empty man, but I have no right to do so, as he is a stranger to me. Between my village and the town with the harbour, a scattering of whitewashed single-storey houses lines the road. In the summers when I am on the island I pass through there a few times a week on my way to the market. When I reach the roundabout just before the houses, I already look out for him. He is part of the order of the universe; if he is not there, something is not right with the world. But he is always there. He sits on a cheap garden chair which has tin arms, faded canvas. He always wears sunglasses, even if the sun is not shining. He sits and watches, or does not watch, the cars that pass by. He is always alone. He does not read, not a book, not a newspaper, not ever. The traffic along that road is busy, and he sits there at all hours, breathing in the exhaust fumes. Always in the same position, whenever I pass by. What is going through his mind? Maybe nothing at all, and that would be the greatest puzzle. I want him to be thinking something, but I cannot imagine what his thoughts might be. A philosopher without a school and without a notebook, obsessed with one eternal, obstinate thought. A poet who is writing inside his head about a man who will never write anything. One day somebody will lift him out of that chair and into a coffin. Where I am now, evening is turning into night. It must be daytime over there, the hours when he sits in his chair, but I cannot ask anyone here if that is so.

SURFACE

The boat is small, in fact more a sort of tub. Two delicately sketched creatures fly through the air above the blue swell of the waves. There are three men in the little vessel, the one at the back has to propel it with a single oar. A fourth man is in the water, but he cannot be swimming, only treading water at most, because he is holding out both hands to a fifth, who is standing on the waves without sinking. The first four men look as anyone should look when they see a man walking on water: big, black pupils in eyes full of amazement and reverence. The name of the man in the water is written beside him: Petrus. The fifth man has a golden halo, his initials appear above him in Greek. Of all the things Poseidon must have seen from the depths, those two foot soles of the Son of the other God on the wrong side of the water's surface must have been the strangest. All five men have their mouths closed, as if they have nothing to say. If there was any sound, it was that of the waves, and of the footsteps on the glistening water.

GREEN

The more we look, the more we know. The more we know, the greater the mystery. When we step out of the domain of science and into the domain of myth, and then step back again so that we can employ the arsenal of myth to look at science, fables come into being of their own accord. Then the Hubble telescope becomes the Cyclops with the biggest eye in the world, peering out far beyond the Pleiades and the Milky Way into magical regions where the universe's meal is being prepared. An entire nation of zeroes is required when speaking about such matters. These distances in time and space defeat the imagination, until a detail becomes stuck in your mind. The photograph in the newspaper is as black as soot. At the top, a catholic turbulence swirls around, an incandescent core surrounded by a wide fan of cardinal's scarlet and episcopal purple, and diagonally beneath it an archipelago in green, the Moluccas or a fragmented Giacometti, call it what you will. It is the green that takes us into the territory of fable. Green is human, spring, there is no need to be frightened of it. The Vatican up at the top had a flickering quasar as its inner sanctum, but 200,000 years ago (what kind of category is that, a year?) a switch was flicked, and we can no longer see the quasar itself. All that remains to us of galaxy IC 2497—which I call the Vatican because of its liturgical aura—is the afterglow, but anyone who has ever been in love knows that can be intense enough. As it is in this case. The cloud of gas flowing from the Vatican catches the last sacred light from the extinguished power source, and has assumed the form of floating islands, or of an equally green atavistic woman with no arms who is spreading her legs over the black sheet of the cosmic night. The greenness of the cloud is due to all the oxygen it contains, but I actually do not wish to know that. They are between 44,000 and 136,000 light years apart, IC 2497 and its green gas cloud, which, perhaps witness to a collision between two galaxies, wraps itself lovingly around the stars. An Ovid should be called upon to describe these love stories, a Poet of the Universe in the service of the universal world government. It was a biology teacher, Hanny van Arkel, from Heerlen in the Netherlands, who discovered this tropically green gas cloud in 2007, when she was contributing to the amateur project Galaxy Zoo. What she saw is now called Hanny's Voorwerp, or Hanny's Object, the shortest poem in the Dutch language, and the one that will probably live the longest.

POSEIDON XV

Death can sometimes be very small, as small as a bird's
wing. I mulled over this thought after rereading the fight
between Aeneas and Achilles in Homer, an insane story
of destruction in which you play a part that I found con-
temptible, even as a schoolboy. Achilles wants to kill
Aeneas, and you prevent him. No big deal for you; you are
a god, and you always have your box of magic tricks with
you. That time, you did it with mist. It is strange that every
age has a past in which the people were stronger. Aeneas
hurls his mighty spear, but the shield that Hephaestus made
for Achilles stops it. Achilles shouts out and lunges with his
sword at Aeneas, who has no weapon now and so grabs a
boulder "a huge great thing, that two men could not carry
between them, of the folk that live now—but he swung
it easily on his own," but then you intervene, the divine
spoilsport, with your impenetrable mist. That fog ensures
that Achilles can no longer see his opponent, but even if he
had been able to, it would not have helped him, because in
one swift movement you pluck Achilles' spear from Aeneas'
shield and lay it at the feet of Achilles, who is standing
dazed in a cloud. You send Aeneas flying through the air

across the entire length of the seething battlefield, the
mêlée of cavalry and infantry, the screaming, the blood
and the dead. When reading the story, all this happens
in a moment of absolute simultaneity, because in those
few seconds, you have already spoken to Hera and Athene,
heard that the two goddesses believe the Trojans should not
be saved from destruction, not even if the Greeks one day
set fire to their city. You do not listen, you believe that your
brother Zeus wants Aeneas to survive "so that the line of
Dardanos should not perish without seed or trace," you
tell Aeneas that from now on he must always avoid fighting with Achilles because he is sure to lose, and then you
are back with Achilles, where you lift the mist, your magic
trick having worked, opponent vanished, saved by a god,
intolerable interference. You will say that Hephaestus also
took sides when he made that shield so completely impenetrable, but a shield is a shield, and mist is mist, and a man
who wishes to kill someone needs his eyes. The hero vents
his frustration in a savage massacre on the banks of the Scamander, the river that is itself a god. The water is red with
blood; bodies and limbs lie all around; the victims float in
the water, which is so full of death that the eels have a feast,
devouring the kidneys and fat of the corpses until the river
can take no more and calls out to Apollo and begs for help.
Achilles hears this and leaps into the river mid-stream, and
it frantically tosses the dead bodies that are choking it up
onto its banks; the water seethes and swirls and becomes
so wild that the hero is sucked in and nearly drowns, a
man battles with a river, a mortal is defeated by a wall of
black water, a hero flees from the river, which pursues him
like an angry hunter, attacking him with wave after wave
whenever he pauses for a moment, until he too calls out

to the gods and you go to him, with Athene, and take him by the hand. I have tried to imagine all this, the wild river, the bodies, you and the other gods constantly interfering in the battle, Hera and her son Hephaestus coming to the aid of Achilles, and setting the river on fire until the divine water begs for mercy. But it is to no avail, his divine water melts like the "lard of a fatted hog" when the fire beneath the pan is stoked high, dissolving and evaporating into steam as dense as the mist that had blinded Achilles. And such is the spectacle: the churned-up soil thick with the dead, the smell of death and destruction, the colour of blood and intestines, groaning and wailing, vultures and rats.

But now the gods too have come to blows: you curse Apollo, who refuses to be provoked, Hera attacks Artemis, Athene cries on Zeus' shoulder, and in the meantime Achilles continues to make corpses, a whole landscape full of them, until for the second time on that endless day he is deceived by a god, as Apollo assumes the form of his last opponent and uses this ruse to lure the hero away from the Trojans that he would still like to kill.

What remains is the battlefield in the slowly encroaching dusk. Now it is still, a stillness in which I read the words told by thousands of mouths, an eternal echo of voices, until someone came along and transformed those sounds into writing that could not be erased, words of destiny and deceit.

And what about my wing? It was lying on the path in my garden. You would recognise the landscape: pine trees and wild olives, stones and dusty soil, with that little wing upon it, a blue one. It was the colour that made me notice it, a deep vibrant blue, a bird I do not know. There is no body attached, just that wing with a small bone, still with a little flesh on it, which is being eaten away by ants, a moving layer of tiny, voracious panzers. The wing lay there almost like a flower, but, like those corpses on the battle-field, it signified death. Around twenty narrow feathers in three shades of blue, folded into a V shape, memento of a battle, already damaged by decay. Big death, small death, as if something were trying to take me back to the words I had just read.

BAL DES AMBASSADEURS

1938, Buenos Aires. Most of the men are dressed in white suits. Some of the women have fancy hats, some do not. War will not come for more than a year, the future enemies are all in the same room, that other continent, the one with the threat, is a journey by ship away. In the foreground, a man alone at a table, his thoughts invisible. The others have stood up to dance, but the music too is inaudible. A man is wearing a cardboard crown, the hair of the man at the next table, who is selecting something from a waiter's tray, gleams with brilliantine. His neighbour is leaning forward so as better to listen to the woman with the long, narrow hands who is sitting diagonally across the table from him, but it is hard to catch her words over the music of what appears to be a slow dance. I cannot hear what she is saying either. I could make something up—that is what I normally do, after all—but it is better this way. I see them from above, a whirl paused in time, their conversations evaporated and dissolved in the anxious air, just as the colour of the flowers has disappeared, and the bodies have been tidied away into graveyards on five continents. If I try very hard, I can hear snatches of words and sentences—Masaryk, Rheinland,

München—but then they fly away or take refuge behind other, more innocent words—foxtrot, tomorrow, champagne, reception—mouths closed or lips parted, sentences in many different languages frozen, together with their meaning, and among the dance steps and the evening wear, the flirtations and the espionage, among those men and women, there is music, and the secret of time.

CIRCE

1829. An army is on the march from Moscow to Arzrum. Bad roads, mud, mire, farewell to Europe. The young poet following the troops in a barouche is called Alexander Pushkin. As they move onwards, the journey becomes more arduous, and his coach is frequently stuck in the sucking mud. Sometimes they travel no more than fifty versts in a day. He notes down what he sees: the forests disappearing, the grass becoming thicker and tougher, the hills giving way to a plain that loses itself in infinity. Herds of wild horses, the oceanic emptiness of Asia, the people who live there, their kibitkas pitched at the stopping places along the endless road. Kalmyks. Their kibitkas, their tents, are made of wicker meshwork covered with white felt. The poet steps out of his barouche and goes into one of those tents. It is early morning, and the Kalmyk family is having breakfast. In the middle of the kibitka is a fire, above it something cooking in a pan. The smoke is drawn up through a hole in the roof of the tent. He sees a girl, perhaps a young woman, who is smoking a pipe as she sews. He sits down beside her. She is beautiful. He asks her name and she tells him, but we are not permitted to know; for the reader, her answer consists of asterisks, three little stars, as he keeps her name to himself, a form of theft. How old are you? Eighteen. What are you making? A pair of trousers. For whom? For myself. She hands him her pipe and begins to eat. A tea of mutton fat and salt. When she offers him a cup, he does not wish to refuse and he takes a sip but tries not to breathe in. He has never smelled anything more repulsive. He asks for something to take the taste away and she gives him a dried piece of mare's flesh. When he has finished eating, he leaves. Intimidated by Kalmyk coquetry, he flees this Circe, and he writes the sentence containing that word: Circe. So she does have a name of sorts. But beyond that? What I read was a moment in time, but what she experienced, the aristocratic gentleman climbing down from his coach and into her tent, has crumbled away, been erased. Why is there no material aspect to thoughts, so that they still exist somewhere? The dark matter of the history of the human species is made up of such moments, invisible, inaudible thoughts that once occurred somewhere, to someone, and which, through the very slowest of summations, have assumed physical form, in a wrinkle, a glance, a position, a tone of voice, because, while things may disappear, they are never gone entirely, a heavy mass of irretrievable thoughts, experiences, silently transmitted presence, for which there is no evidence at all.

Eight years after he wrote those words, he was killed in a duel. We know no more about her than what he wrote, that she was beautiful, a girl, a pipe, a tent, the three stars of her name, now gone for good.

HARBOUR

My island lies between Spain and Italy in the Mediterranean Sea. A shepherd from Sardinia, a swineherd from Ithaca, a fisherman from Corfu, they would recognise everything: the sound of the waves, the untouchable thistles, the ochre of the lichen on the battered rocks, the taste of the figs, the sudden storms, the antiquity of the stories that have blown from coast to coast, the fish and the shells that have the same forms everywhere, and everywhere different names. As I am writing, I am looking at an incredibly finely etched map from 1786, when the British had just been driven out, but had left their forts behind. It shows the largest harbour on the island, a long, deep gullet full of names and numbers, depths and mooring places, a strategic location in a sea that was the centre of the world, both colony and battlefield. Everyone was here, Phoenicians, Iberians, Romans, Arabs, Jews, but no matter who came, they all found the constructions made by those other people, the ones who lived here before Homer wrote down the names of gods and heroes for the first time. They did not leave behind any writings, but they did leave the things that they built using what everyone finds here in the island's soil: stone. When I look outside, I see the walls that have been built around my piece of land, which appear to have stood there for hundreds of years, walls made of loose, light-grey stones with no cement between them, the most peculiar shapes, a stack of large and smaller pieces of rock that the builders join together as if they were soft clay, but which were once forcibly hewn from the hard soil upon which my house stands. Billions of stones must have been pulled out of the ground here, as every plot on the island is surrounded by these walls, and so they seem like some late echo of the prehistoric structures in which those strangers lived their mysterious lives: their communal houses, burial chambers, temple-like construc- tions, where huge blocks of stone have been lifted on top of one another and yet no-one knows how.

We do not know whom they worshipped either, but we do know that the dimensions of the stones suggest some knowledge of mathematical principles, an awareness of proportions and harmony. It is uncertain whether these megalithic monuments also had astrological significance, but anyone who has ever stood at night beside one of these talayots or taulas and beneath the filled pages of the book of heaven can have no doubt. They were followed by the palaeo-Christian basilicas, the temples, the mosques, the synagogues, a landscape of memories, a bastion of immeasurable antiquity that had to protect itself from hostile strangers and pirates, a coast bristling with round watchtowers where fires were lit when danger threatened or unknown ships were sighted, passing their message of impending doom from tower to tower with smoke in the daytime and fire at night. When I think of this island, I imagine a mighty ship of stone, but when I look at that old map of the largest natural harbour in the Mediterranean, it seems more like a prehistoric monster with a horn on its forehead and another on the back of its head, allowing it to attack in both directions. Throughout the long years I have been here, I have become familiar with every inch of those horns and I know what they look like in reality: hard, dry earth on a precipitous coast. The monster's maw is a narrow one, large ships have to manoeuvre carefully here, and on either side are the forts of the Spaniards and the British with their now impotent cannon. I read the names of the islands in the harbour, King's Island, Quarantine Island, the inlet of the Greeks, and then, more distant, the cove of San Esteban, the bay of Bini Saida, the island of the Air. There are tents and fortifications on the map, army units of Catalans and dragoons, batteries and monasteries, scarps and orchards, the old roads along which I still walk, between hills that are etched in the finest of lines. Everything has a story to tell of battles, sieges, defeats, death and destruction. Shouts and whispers in all of the languages ever spoken here, always drowned out by the sound of the sea, over which enemies arrived and departed, came and stayed, the story of an island.

POSEIDON XVI

We have adopted some of your privileges. We can fly. We can hear the voices of the dead, speak to people on the other side of the world, see the palaces of our enemies from the air and send that image to our allies, we can look inside the brain and see where the memory lives—all things that you would have called a miracle. We know which acids are responsible for our perceptions, that fear cannot be detached from the sensations of the body, and not from the mind either, which uses the body as its theatre—and the strange thing is that everything we know also applies to you. You are, after all, a god in human form, so nothing human can be strange to you, except for illness and death. We have named all of these things with words from your language: chaos, physics, thermodynamics, psyche, neurons, laws that you did not yet know, but sometimes suspected. Do you remember the sacrifices that people once made to you? At least you appreciated them. You wanted to spare Aeneas because he made gifts that were pleasing to the gods. That is why you argued with Apollo and why you came to Aeneas' assistance when Achilles was about to kill him. Do you still remember all of that? The sacrifices? The aroma of ox meat roasting over a fire, the sheer delight? The smell of the wood when it started to burn? A wide beach, your sea beyond, the fires, the oxen slowly turning, the pleasure of anticipation, kindled by that aroma? Air circulates through the mouth and rises up through the nose, where the minuscule gaseous particles that are generated as the meat roasts find their way to the ten million receptors that are situated in the nose within an area the size of a thumb print. Yes, even in *your* nose, although you did not know that. Then a surge of ionic energy is generated, which travels through the ivory edifice of the skull and seeks out the brain. Yes, that includes yours, too. Did you need to know that, in such detail? Perhaps not. Plato, Gorgias, Virgil and Erasmus had no idea about it either, and they did not complain. Lucretius had a suspicion, but he had no way of knowing the exact pathways of the brain–body connection, any more than you did. But once you are aware of the secret marriage that constantly occurs within us, of the nerves and their song in voltages, of the entire electrical system within the body, the magical processes of our existence, the soul that consists of flesh and perishes along with it, the contradiction of our remarkable presence, then even as a god surely you can only marvel?

A sense of amazement: a gift. Perhaps even the gift that brought about your creation. But, as I said, of course I do not know if you want to hear all that.

P.S. I cannot leave it at that. So how does that ionic energy get into my brain, you will wonder. Or you *might* wonder. I have no idea what you think about all this. Not everyone wishes to see his own body from the inside, let alone get lost within the labyrinth of his own brain. And yet, I have seen the answer. Yes, we can do that. We are mortal, fleeting, but powerful. The scent particle travels along an axon. You must remember that word; it comes from your own language and means "axis." A thread-like, fibrous axis at the tip of a neuron, which conducts electrical impulses. They can be over a metre long. I do not wish to bore you any further, just to tell you that these are inner landscapes of great beauty. Magnify a neuron (we can do everything, or almost everything, even feats that once only gods could accomplish, such as making objects larger and smaller) and you will see a hazy landscape of frayed lines, branches of trees in the mist; it is autumn there, and if you look closely you can see me walking, without an umbrella, even though it looks like rain. I am magnified four hundred times. 688 metres tall; if I meet Polyphemus, I will swat him away, no matter if he is your son one hundred times over. But perhaps instead I should be reduced by a factor of four hundred to fit into the landscape inside my head.

HIPPOPOTAMUS

Some day or other, some place or other. By which I mean that I could have been someone else, in another city, on another day. But it is now, here, on the other side of the world, August and winter. The bar is called Hippopotamus, and a stone example of that species, the size of a large dog, stands on a platform at its centre, white and gleaming. It is the kind of space that once existed in Europe, a place for reading, thinking, imagining, where men would plan a revolution and start a literary magazine. It is grey outside. At a distant table, someone is writing, but that is me. The number 29 bus goes past, as it does in so many other cities. Here, it is purple. Across the road is another bar. I do not know why I did not choose to sit there. It is a mirror image of this bar, so perhaps I am sitting there, too. Through the window I see a park, a heroic statue, tall trees that do not lose their leaves in the local winter. The waiters are in black, with long black aprons, as if they are in mourning. There are ten men in the bar, three women. On the wall is a slightly tilted mirror, in which the world outside is reflected again, but as an inclined plane. The headlines in the news-paper on the table beside me shout about the infernal jig of the stock exchange. The road surface in front of the bar is made of cobblestones with, between them, tram rails sealed with asphalt. The tram must once have turned here, but now the rails end in nothingness. And yet I can hear the sound of that defunct tram coming around the corner, a sound in sepia. A man with a short black beard comes into the bar. He could have committed a murder an hour ago. Three other men stand up, and he hugs them, one by one. I do not know why, but I see that as a good sign. Someone phones the woman in blue; she holds a hand up to one side of her mouth, so that no-one in the bar can hear what she is saying. I am always somewhere else. The two young men who have been playing cards behind me all this time now leave. When it is my turn to go and I look back at my empty chair, there can be no certainty that I ever sat there.

HESIOD

He truly believed it, the poet who was a peasant, a shepherd. What kind of day was it, the day that would be so different from any other? I know the image from Spain, where you still see it sometimes: a shepherd with his sheep. They are walking up a low hill, the man off to one side with his stick, the flock with their heads down, chewing on the straw-coloured grass, changing the colour of the meadow as they slowly advance, the red soil becoming visible, with rust now the dominant shade. The colour of sheep and lambs stands out against the slope; the shepherd's eye follows the dog as it runs in wide circles around the flock; this is what they know, a movement in the wide landscape that mimics eternity, days as repetition of themselves, sheep, shepherd, dog, the longest meal, to which no end can ever come, food changing position with infinite slowness, space as a clock with its only hand the *here* that the flock is passing. And then, one day, it happens. The shepherd who was a poet wrote about it in an alphabet that I can still read; he writes that the muses appeared to him, there, at the foot of Mount Helicon, while he was grazing his sheep. These women, daughters of a god, own that great and holy mountain, and he knows who they are, untouchable, holy themselves, they dance on soft feet around the violet-dark fountain and the altar of Zeus; they may draw close to the holiest of holies. There are nine of them, they stand around him in the field, the sound of their voices is not of this world, they sing about Zeus, who is their father, about Artemis, Poseidon, the dawn, the sun, the moon, about the black night, which he knows better than anyone as he sleeps with his flock and listens to the mysterious sounds of the invisible life around him. A laurel tree stands at the edge of the field and, as lightly as creatures with no mass, they danced over to it with the shepherd in their midst, plucked a branch and gave it to him, and at that moment, as he pauses with the still-fragrant branch in his hands, he feels that their breath has created a divine poem that he must now say aloud, a poem about the gods who "always are" and about the women surrounding him, always about the women, first and last.

It is this poem that I am reading now, at an hour between late afternoon and early evening. The sea is restless, the bay empty, the rocks where I am sitting still have the glow of the sun in them. The landscape across the water is his landscape, it is the same sea; the water at this hour is the same violet-dark as it was back then. I read the words in the characters that once, more than sixty years ago, I learned, and I still recognise words, turns of phrase. His poem is almost three thousand years old, but he would still recognise everything here, the way the evening slowly shifts to darkness, the motion and the sound of the water as the sea flows into the strait of the bay, the waves as a slow, surging, never-ending recitation of light and dark sentences that now accompany his poem. Perhaps it is because there is no-one else around, but a strange holiness seems to cling to everything, as if for just one moment it were possible that the time between then and now has dissolved, and that all of it is true: the shepherd who became a poet, the freshly cut laurel branch, the women moving in a circle around him, the book that he would write, the dispute of the gods, their confusing love affairs and cruel secrets, the words that I read until the darkness erases them, words that I keep for the light of the day when they will be written anew for the one who reads them.

POSEIDON XVII

Every sea belongs to you, or so I assume, but I do not know if you would recognise this one. The water looks like molten lead, dangerous. It would like to move, but is barely able. The heat is breath-taking, literally. I have crossed the road to the monument: a flight of birds that wants to rise in a straight line into the sky. The bushes around it are hard, dry, with big leaves. I pick one to keep. A few stones have broken away from the monument; everything here is dilapidated.

The Spanish poem on the pedestal's marble plaque is scarcely legible; it describes a moment, the swoop of an *alcatraz* plunging into the sea and breaking through the glass of the mirror to come back up with a fish. Death in the afternoon. An *alcatraz* is a gannet, but that name seems out of keeping in this place. I look at the poem, and then at the sea, and I see what I am reading: a winged weapon hurtling down, piercing your surface, returning with its offering, which briefly flashes white in this new light. Did you see it? Do you see everything, like that God of ours, without whose knowledge no sparrow falls to the ground? This is not the sea of Ithaca; the gold of Indian gods was transported over this sea to another continent for a war that was also about a god, our god, the One True God, the one with the capital letter. You gods are a demanding kind, always appearing in different guises, never satisfied with what you receive, destroying and usurping one another, sucking away at the addictive prayers of humankind.

The leaf I picked is here beside me now, it is hard and green and round, with veins the colour of blood. I do not speak its language and yet I know what it says.

QUILOTOA

Forgetting is the absent brother of Memory, an ill-matched pair who take a very casual approach to ruling over what we believe is our property. Memory is, after all, something that we ourselves have gathered and recorded and when we lose our memories it is as if something has been stolen from us. Perhaps it is the cold, perhaps the altitude of the barren mountain landscape, but suddenly I remember something that once, a lifetime ago, I had hidden in my memory palace (Augustine) and not found since. It involves Theseus, and perhaps what actually prompted the thought here, at almost four thousand metres, is the narrow path around the sharp, serrated edge of the vast crater of Quilotoa where I have spent the past hour, transfixed by the lake in its depths, which the local people say has no bottom. As I gaze at the perfectly still, blue metallic surface, I believe all of the stories. Theseus had agreed with his best friend Pirithous that they would abduct Helen, the most beautiful of all women, and then free Persephone, the wife of Hades, the god of the underworld, from the darkness of the realm of the dead. They had formed a holy alliance and to seal it they had carved their agreement in the lip of a volcano.

And of course I now think that it was this volcano, here in this deserted region of Ecuador that Humboldt called the Avenue of the Volcanoes. I have never seen quite so much lip; it would take six hours to walk all the way around it. Humboldt must once have stood where I am now standing, and little can have changed since then.

The road to this place passes through pastoral landscapes: shabby dwellings at the foot of tanned mountains, terraces where people struggle to cultivate a few scanty crops, strange, abrupt hills truncated at the top by a field of maize—who knows how anyone gets up there? Near the crater is one last house, where you can have a coffee. A local woman, an iron stove, wood, ash, warmth at last, a copper kettle, silence. Outside, icy wind, a donkey, a few men, and then the crater. I trusted to luck when I started walking, and now I can see paths leading down to the depths, but I want to remain up above and look out through the grass and lupins at the relentlessly steep wall opposite, where the black volcanic rock of the crater stands vertically in water where no fish can live, and I think that the entrance to the underworld must be here, the opening into which Theseus descended with his friend and was received by Hades—who was friendly, of course, because everyone is welcome in the realm of the dead. Poseidon's brother offers the young men two stone chairs, but when they sit down they stick to the seats and, with no way of standing up again, they dream as if they have drunk from the water of Lethe, and they forget everything. Their lives are erased, the sound of their names disappears, what they had wanted to do no longer exists; this is the realm of the dead, the eternal fog in which everything is forgotten. It will be Hercules who rescues Theseus, but Pirithous still sits there in total oblivion;

that last detail is what once made such a strong impression on me in a classroom at my monastery school. The Greek teacher was a monk whom we called Pa; I can no longer remember why, perhaps it was an abbreviation of *pater*. He had difficulty speaking, his words came out as reverse sighs, aspirated, as if he were sucking in air and the strange inverted commas that indicate an "h" in front of a Greek word had become part of his being. The power of stories, and of remembering, of wresting something from oblivion. As I walk away I look back at the edge of the crater to see if their oath is still carved there, but all I see is a light mist advancing slowly over the entire landscape, veiling the minuscule figures down below, beside the water, the size of their bodies indicating the size of the world.

THUNDERSTORM

It happens once a year on this island, the big storm. The power cut is part of it, and when evening comes we are vulnerable creatures who live with candles, an impotent form of fire that is no match for the biting white light outside. Everything vibrates; it was at such a moment that someone beside this sea dreamed up a god and gave him the name Earth-Shaker. A crazed drummer, in his frenzy, has switched off everything: the television, the radio, the refrigerator, the computer. Everyday life has become void and ridiculous. We have new masters now, and they have capital letters: Rain, Wind, Lightning, kings that Nature keeps up her sleeve as a violent reminder of who is in charge. The rain stabs down with vertical knives, you can hear the water swirling along the gutters; the wind whips the palms and the oleasters with great lashes, and they become instruments of a wild rage, their usual shapes ripped apart, torn away, unravelled; this is no longer a noise but a death scream. The worst is the lightning, combined with the ancient force of the thunder, inscribing a coded text across the heavens in shifting Gothic runes; if we could read them they would say something about impotence and animal fear, about danger.

It is electricity itself that wishes to tell us something about our limitations, that is writing the possibility of a dreadful fate for us in icy white, condemning us to read in fear, to be aware of our absolute dependence. When it is over, I drive through large puddles to the coast, where the surf rages at the rocks. The distant writer is far from finished with his work, his most recent messages appear above the horizon where the other, invisible islands must be: we have not heard the last of him, he will spare us this time, but he can always return, a cruel and unapproachable master who knows where we live.

ZOO

We know about impossible love between people, but other laws hold sway between animals, and so their love remains a mystery, if only because they do not write about it. It is late afternoon in this city, where the animals fare little better than the people. Decay, torn-up pavements, rubbish everywhere, cleaned away and immediately replenished. The animals do not seem too bothered. Their cages are old, the bars rusty, the imitation rocks filthy and peeling, the water dark and murky. The polar bear looks surprisingly white against its shabby backdrop, but I know that the hairs of its coat are not in fact white, but transparent, so as to catch what little sunlight there is in the high North. The condor hangs like a tattered rag beneath its sky of iron mesh, refusing to spread its mighty wings; the white lions lean against one another and look right through us. Eagles, lions, tigers, I walk among these living heraldic emblems, see the hippopotamus from yesterday's bar as a version of itself magnified one hundred times, a survivor. These animals can no longer exist, it is an impossible task, their huge bodies are more ephemeral than a sparrow's, they have no place here. Whenever the world becomes too much for me,

I have to visit the animals; the clear, intrusive gaze of human beings glances off their impenetrability. Look into an owl's eyes for five minutes and you are no longer certain who you are. I watch my temporary contemporaries using their mobile phones to take pictures of the tiger's eternal circuits and know that the secret of that nerve-ridden lockstep will no longer be visible when they get home. Fat rodents scurry over the paths—I do not know what they are called, some kind of giant marmot—they are searching for something among the pebbles and the grass with their distinguished, nervous faces. Why did I come here? The lion, sprawling on his lawn, has dispensed with the world; he sleeps within his own coat of arms. A white heron in a palm tree, part of a story I have never heard. I would like to walk around here at night, when they are all sleeping, or not sleeping. What would they see, the anteater, the sloth, the monkey? A solitary human being, pacing up and down behind his bars, the great role reversal. Where the path turns, there is a small cage with a fake mountain landscape. It is a moment before I spot her: a black cat. We eye each other. Just an ordinary cat, says a passer-by to his daughter. The sign on the bars says that if you look closely you can see the markings on her coat underneath all that blackness. I do not see anything. Mountain cat, *gato montanes*. She looks like all the other black cats I have ever seen, but if I stroked her, she would bite. Those greenish eyes lock onto mine; she knows I would like to place a chair in front of her cage and watch her for hours. A mechanical voice floats above the cages: the zoo will close in half an hour. The *dierentuin* in my language: the animal garden. You just have to split a word in two to hear it properly for the first time: animal garden, garden with animals. I head to where I think the exit is and

I see the high heads of two giraffes in the distance. If you take human beings as the standard measure, creatures with a head, a mouth, with legs, ears, eyes, hands, and you see in those beaks, paws, tusks and muzzles the same systems of grasping, looking, listening, eating, both the connection and the disconnect become increasingly clear. Perhaps that closeness and that distance are what brings me here. If I drop onto all fours, if my arms are stretched until they are longer than my legs, if I remove my clothes and my skin is covered with short gleaming hair in strange patterns that no-one has drawn, and if someone else comes along and stretches my neck to infinite heights, so that I, just like the two creatures before me, have my head above the crowd, and sail past people like some great ship, then I will no longer be able to write, but perhaps I will know the delightful sensation that must occupy that little head: constant, quiet amazement at the peculiar commotion down below.

But then it happens, an image of impossible love. A zebra is licking the wooden palisade that separates the giraffes' enclosure from its own. One of the giraffes bends that inconceivably long neck over the fence and seeks out the zebra, far down below. What follows is a caress, and a form of kissing. Their markings clash and yet they merge. Love. The zebra licks the long neck, the giraffe's face rubs the zebra's striped cheek. Then the giraffe extricates itself, walks some distance away across the desert-coloured sand of its own territory, and returns. The zebra has remained there, waiting. As soon as the giraffe's head reappears, high above her, she raises her own head and the petting begins again, their lips touch. I stand there until the final call and I think about my next visit. In foreign cities, one needs to have fixed points.

POSEIDON XVIII

I attempt to picture the scene. You saw Alope, the daughter of Cercyon, a king of Eleusis, blue eyes, blonde, dancing in the meadow, a deer. Kings everywhere, daughters and innocence everywhere, and always your unbridled lust. How you gods managed to keep your relationships untangled is another puzzle, because Cercyon was a son of Hephaestus, who was in turn one of your brother's sons, born after a wedding night of four hundred years. Nothing is ever too far-fetched or outlandish in your perpetual mating dance. You find her attractive, you want her, have her, a child is born, one of your countless sons and daughters, divine and otherwise; much of humanity descends from you gods through such chains of events. Cercyon knows nothing about the child, Alope is scared of her father, gives the child to a wet-nurse who is to leave it exposed on a mountain somewhere. Of course it is found—or there would be no story. Hyginus, who wrote it all down, knew his craft. A mare suckles the child, a shepherd sees it and takes the child in its princely gown to the stable—after all, one never knows if one might have found a royal child, and shepherds too are aware of the conventions of storytelling. Another shepherd wishes to bring up the baby, but he also wants to have the gold brocade, as royal lineage requires proof. So there is a dispute between the two shepherds, but in those days kings were not as busy, and so the shepherds are called before Cercyon to settle their argument. Kings recognise royal fabrics, they too know how stories are written, the wet-nurse is made to confess, Cercyon has Alope locked up and, once again, the child is left to die. Do you ever think about all the trouble you have caused? All those desperate stories that always end in some kind of metamorphosis, with nature being required to solve the problem for you. The mare gets to suckle the child for the second time and this time it is found by the second shepherd, who gives the baby a name: Hippothoon. So that is one of your sons. Yours and Alope's, who has in the meantime died in jail without you ever extending a divine helping hand. She does not receive a decent burial either, but is shoved into the ground somewhere on the road between Eleusis and Megara, in the place where Cercyon held his wrestling matches. Only then do you take action and grant a divine pittance: you transform the body you once desired, turning it into a spring. A poor reward for services rendered, or do you think being a spring such a marvellous boon? Sometimes I cannot reconcile all of these stories, not with the marble statue beside the Arsenal in Venice, not with the mighty figure with the trident on all of those paintings by the great masters, not with the hurricane of fury with which you pursued Odysseus for all those years, with which you ravaged coasts across the entire world, and continue to do so, even today. When I think of you with all those nymphs and moon maidens, what I picture is something more like the frivolous portrait that Kees van Dongen painted of himself in what he believed was your guise: a young, lusty Polynesian covered with necklaces and shells, a strange pilgrim with cockleshells around his slim waist, an olive-skinned inhabitant of Oceania, that at least is true, off in search of kings' daughters to use and then abandon somewhere in the form of a spring. Now, of course, I will have to take care next time I go for a swim in the sea, but someone had to speak up for Alope, and I could picture her before me.

LIVES

When can someone be said to have existed? Such a question does not apply to gods, of course, who, as Hesiod so clearly expressed it, "always are." No, this time it is about humans, mortals, transient creatures that live longer than flowers or insects but shorter than some tortoises. Most people have existed because they have lived. This means that they have existed for themselves and for those around them, but when they are no longer around and those who knew them have died, usually no memory of them remains. I shall leave aside the issue of how bad that might be. There have been billions of people, priests in ancient Greece, prisoners of the Aztecs, Egyptian civil servants, hunters in fifteenth-century Austria, monks in the Spanish colonies, victims of earthquakes, soldiers in the Boer War, about whom we know that they existed as a type, but generally not as an individual. Does that matter? Does it change anything about the validity of their lives? Was it any less of a real life because we know nothing about it, because we do not know their names and have no idea where their graves might be? For those people themselves, there was only that life from birth to death, an existence of happiness

or misery, excitement or boredom, on the edge of histori-
cal events or in the midst of them. So they did not write
their name in the book of history, which is read less and
less these days anyway, but again, does that matter? Does
it matter that they have not invented anything, not written
a book, not committed a gruesome murder? No, so why is
it that I am thinking today about a hump-backed duchess,
who was such a good dancer, about an outrageous marquis,
about an unpleasant duke who lost the power of speech on
the Pont Royal on his way to a party on Shrove Tuesday
and died shortly afterwards on the toilet, with his face con-
torted into a terrible grimace?

How does such a thing happen? It is late in the evening
and I open one of the many volumes of the memoirs of the
Duke of Saint-Simon at a random page, a random year, in
this case 1710, life at the court of Louis XIV, world politics,
courtly intrigue, issues of power and rank, backbiting, all
captured by that merciless pen, as he ruthlessly exposes the
people he characterises in just a handful of sentences, making them emerge from the darkness of oblivion as living
creatures. With a few strokes of the pen he commemorates
three people who had died in rapid succession: the Duchess of Foix was the "prettiest hunchback imaginable,"
the Marquis of Courcillon was "a man like no other . . .
He made grim jokes whilst they amputated his leg after
the Battle of Malplaquet," Monsieur le Duc was "very
considerably shorter than the shortest men, and without
being fat was thick throughout; his head was astonishingly
thick, and his face was frightening . . . His skin was a livid
yellow, his expression seldom free from anger, and always
so bold and so arrogant that it was hard to grow accustomed to him. He possessed wit and learning, the remains

of a good education, and could when so disposed be civil; but that was rare indeed." I hear the furious scratching of a pen on hand-made paper; they have been etched in words and described. For a brief moment I was in 1710 and I saw them, three unexpected contemporaries, with a hump, an amputated leg and the grimace of sudden death.

BULL

Ninety people, half-naked, their bodies painted red; together they form a bull. They are lying on a floor of pale bricks in Cali, Colombia, as the legs, the back, the huge body, the head and the horns of a bull, red with blood. The two most distant bodies are the horns. I have no idea how long the ninety people have been lying there, that is not clear from the photograph. Some of them have their legs wide open, others are holding their head in their arms, the bull's legs are lying with their heads towards the stomach, while the stomach parts have their heads towards the feet of the back section; it cannot have been pleasant. It is as if some strange form of organised disaster has struck these people, and so it does not resemble the iconography of daily violence on our front pages: an Afghan massacre or the aftermath of a suicide bomb in Pakistan. These ninety living people depict the atavistic form of a dead animal, they have laid down their bodies in an orderly fashion, and I believe them: the ninety bodies have become a dead animal. Around where the neck bones must be, some rather frivolous coloured paper lies between two arms, intended to represent the *banderillas*, those vicious, decorated barbs that the flying matador hooks into the neck to agitate the bull. They have to be firmly rammed home so that they dance along with his furious leaps. When the photograph was taken, it must have been very still: a dead bull does not move. I look again at the power in the head, and then at the horns. Using a human body to depict the curved horn of a bull is no easy task. I try to imagine what would happen if this bull were to join together all of his ninety bodies and stand up, and what the Theseus might look like who would have the task of killing that bull all over again.

POSEIDON XIX

Nothing. Nothing is happening at all. I walked out of a film because I could predict the ending and now my universe looks like a bar in Buenos Aires whose name I do not know. Dishes are written on a board in chalk, but I am not hungry. Outside, heavy traffic is racing past, buses and taxis along the Avenida del Libertador. So everything outside is as it should be. It is seven fifty-seven in the evening, and winter here, so it is dark. I see the lights of a train and then those of a large aeroplane taking off. The woman at the next table reads *La Nación* and then *Clarín*, the clarion. In the mirror on the wall, I see one of those televisual marriages of opportunity, a man and a woman who do not belong together in real life but who meet every day to report the news of the world, battlefields, bodies, ministers, protest marches, burning cars, football, the inimitable theatrics of the stock exchanges. Their mouths are moving, but their voices cannot be heard. I look at the large white face of the clock and see the thin second hand moving with small, measured jumps that have the rhythm of a heartbeat. Yesterday, news came that a friend had died. I think of his body now lying in some funeral home on the other side of the world.

He was always a well-mannered man and so he died at his small desk on the ground floor of his old Amsterdam house. If death had surprised him upstairs, they would have needed to winch him to ground level. The proportions of his body were at odds with his love for the most fragile antique glass. I occasionally think that I live longer so that I can mark the deaths of some of my friends. Someone once wrote that I travel so much in order to escape death. So clearly he did not understand. We cannot escape death, not our own, and not that of our friends, no matter where we are. Only gods are immortal, although I have my doubts about that. I do not like to say that to you, but you never answer anyway; it is your best quality. The woman who was reading the newspaper has gone. Now that she is no longer there, I have an unobstructed view of a younger woman with red hair, who is reading a book. You would have wanted her and had her, just as you had everyone you wanted, Alope and all those others. Even if you had to change yourself into a stallion to do so, as you did with Demeter. The redhead has woven a kind of tower into her hair, temporary architecture which makes her look rather like a priestess. She is sitting beneath the mirror, so I see that fragile tower in duplicate. You would have used her and then turned her into a spring or a star. She has slim hands, like Alope. Do not ask me how I know that. I leave her alone with her author's words, and transform her into words she will never read. Was it love, with Alope, or was it a rape garnished with flattery, the perverse privilege of the gods? Bus 92, bus 101, the black and orange of the minicabs in the icy neon of the street lamps, images of war, snatches of music and carefree voices, a man in black with a white plastic bag, and the seventh aeroplane, a dead friend far away. No, nothing is happening, nothing at all.

SISTERS

It happens every autumn. Black worms on my white walls, elongated glyphs on a blank sheet. They come alone, and so create no words or sentences, just that single, stretched-out letter of flesh, desperately trying to mean something. Flesh is a euphemism; it has to be something like that, but that is not how it seems. They feel hard, plastic, as if they were made in a factory somewhere. I am not sure if the birds like them or not. I suspect the worms would not make themselves so available if that were the case. I hold them between thumb and index finger, the worm struggles to curl up, but I can feel that he or she is actually too stiff to do so. I come across a few of them every day, their mournful message expressing a longing for death, but no matter how closely I study them, I cannot detect any form of sadness. I do not know where they spend the rest of the year, or whether they have ever been fat and juicy, a tasty meal for the black-birds that have already departed. For me, they belong with the snails that will arrive as soon as it rains, and with the dark black-and-red glow of the admiral, which lands on the same cluster of *Aeonium* every year to remind me of mortality. "Every globe has its distinctive economy and laws and products," wrote Charles Bonnet in 1764, and he went on: "There are perhaps worlds so imperfect relatively to ours, that there are to be found in them only . . . [inanimate] beings. Other worlds, on the contrary, may be so perfect that there are in them only beings of the superior classes. In these latter worlds, the rocks are organic bodies, the plants have sensation, the animals reason, the men are angels."

They devoted plenty of thought to this subject in the eighteenth century. Kant did not claim that all celestial bodies were inhabited by sentient beings, but he was certain that life and thought could not be limited to the earth, and that such wretched creatures as human beings could not be the best that Nature was capable of producing. Joseph Addison went a step further. He saw the human being as a connection between the spiritual and animal worlds, and therefore said: "So that he, who in one Respect is associated with Angels and Arch-Angels, may look upon a Being of Infinite Perfection as his Father, and the highest order of Spirits as his Brethren, may, in another Respect, say to Corruption, Thou art my Father, and to the Worm, Thou art my Sister." This is why I always pick up my sisters so gently when they arrive to announce that autumn is here. I briefly hold their mournful, hard, glyph-like little bodies in my fingers and lay them tenderly among the bushes for the voracious ants. Rest in peace. In the end, there is always someone who loves you.

WHALE

A whale weighs more than a hundred tonnes, as much as a decent-sized ship, but this ship is made of meat, and meat is mortal. What is it that kills a whale? Exhaustion on those oceanically long journeys, old age, hunger. What happens when a whale dies? A big ship sinks to the bottom of the ocean, sometimes thousands of metres deep. And then the great funeral repast begins. It can last a hundred years, with thousands of guests of different ranks and provenance. What they have in common is hunger. There is not much to eat down there in the darkness. Small organic particles percolate downwards from the unseen surface that the whale has now left behind, and that is usually all, which explains the excitement at the prospect of this meal. The guests, most of whom do not wish to become acquainted, sometimes work together for an entire century to create a bewildering work of funerary art, a scattered collection of giant bones, the abandoned skeleton of a sea giant who was once thirty metres long, the memory of a meal enjoyed in cold, silent depths by funeral guests who are both gravediggers and cemetery. By the end of the feast, all those years later, most of the guests have themselves passed away. Not everyone lives the same length of time; not everyone gets the same to eat. It must be a breathtaking sight. Slowly, the great corpse descends into the growing darkness below, rocked by the movement of the sea. It sways like a tiny dancer in a choreography of death, gravity and currents, until finally it touches the bottom. The bell for dinner consists of an odour of pestilence, a wave of tainted water spreading out in every direction. Sharks and corpse-eating eels are the first guests, along with almost forty species of shellfish and other kinds of fish, carapaced creatures with hooks and claws, everyone who can survive at great depths comes to call, eating their way through blubber and the decay of soft flesh until they can eat no more, this first course lasts for months, and if it is an adult blue whale it can even take a decade, time does not matter down there. Neither does etiquette, the Rabelaisian diners spill their food, gulp it down the wrong way, puke, shit, morsels fall down between the chairs, where another party of guests is already waiting for the next course: worms, slugs, crustaceans eat their fill of the organic wealth of rotting meat, sludge and bacteria. They have travelled dozens of miles, because again time does not matter. As the meal progresses, mating and childbirth goes on, and a new generation of offspring floats onwards in search of the next corpse; almost seventy thousand whales die each year and everyone down there knows the routes taken by the great living battleships and is aware of their mortality. It is just a question of biding time and surviving, and the bone-eating worms that have waited for the skeleton know that too: patience is everything. They secrete large amounts of mucus that feasts on the whalebones and the miraculous oil inside them; they resemble tiny crimson palm trees and have a green root system that can hollow out the whalebone; they even have their own bacteria farm to break down the miracle oil, which makes this worm the first of the guests capable of demolishing those fatty whalebones at the bottom of the ocean and extracting the rich nourishment inside (60 per cent fat, which is why whales are such nifty swimmers). Is that all? No, there is still a dessert course to come, and the bacteria arrive for this, first a party of oxygen-breathing guests, and when the oxygen has all gone—which does not take long—others come, who can breathe sulphate, and who transform the sulphate of the seawater into nutritious sulphide, a feast for a different kind of participant in this communion, small mussels and large clams call in for their share of the bacchanal, which now becomes a full-blown chemistry lesson: four hundred other species live in and around the whale's skeleton for years. Anyone who kills a whale and takes it home destroys the harmony of the food chain. The image of this holy communion that remains with me is a white, snow-coloured veil of bacteria over the dramatic sculpture of the disintegrated skeleton, the final course, which seems to have no end, a sacrificial meal in the ruins of a collapsed cathedral. If what Kafka says is true, the divine bookkeeper with the trident has kept track of it all. No wonder he prefers to stay down below.

BLUE

In 1963, Brigitte Bardot is still beautiful. Her skin gleams sensually, but her face is not good at contempt. Jack Palance has a sports car that is too small and too red for a film mogul, and Michel Piccoli still cannot understand why his wife holds him in contempt, even though it is perfectly obvious that he is selling his talent to Palance's vulgar producer. Fritz Lang functions as an intellectual counterweight, reciting, with a German sense of rhetoric, a passage from the 26th canto of the *Inferno*, in which Odysseus appears as a flame. Piccoli demonstrates his credentials by recognising the quote as lines by Dante, but it is unlikely that he will prove capable of writing a screenplay for Fritz Lang for his movie adaptation of the *Odyssey*, the theme of the film I am now watching, far too late, in 2012: *Le Mépris*, or *Contempt*. He is too light for the task, this Piccoli, still so young, and he also wears a black hat throughout the entire film, which will only really serve him well when Bardot and Palance have met their deaths beneath a giant truck in the little red car. Odysseus, the hero of Lang's film that will never be completed, walks around in a peculiar costume from a theatrical supplier, a few extras intended to represent the chorus wander among marble columns wearing the kind of robes that, since the eighteenth century, have passed for Greek. The three protagonists struggle on laboriously in a drama that never, for a single moment, assumes the inescapable and un-deniable aroma of genuine antiquity; the only real things we see are a classical statue of Athene, and a mighty Poseidon against the backdrop of his own blue sea. The setting is Erich Maria Remarque's futurist villa on Capri, and almost half a century after the film was made I am watching it for the first time because I have read in Anne Carson that Poseidon is κυανο-χαι της, that he has very dark-blue hair, and because someone has told me that the colour blue is also associated with the god in this movie. It was both true and not true. Once, when the god is shown in all his might as the sculpted enemy of Odysseus, it is not his hair but his lips and his blind eyes that are coloured a virulent, luminous, all-penetrating blue, the colour of his sea, just as Tiberius must always have seen it here on Capri, the blue of the epithet attached to the name of the sea god like a Homeric shadow, going wherever he goes, the byname as an eternally faithful hound, until the very end.

POSEIDON XX

When was it, last year, the year before? I was standing in front of the Arsenal in Venice, looking at your statue. You nearly always stand slightly turned away in your statues, looking to one side, as though you wish to avoid a conversation. Would I dare speak to you if I had encountered you there in the same form, but in the flesh? Does one walk up to a man who is standing half-naked in front of a neo-classical gate with a trident on his shoulder and ask him a question? And if so, how should he be addressed? In the Italian of the Renaissance? In Homeric Greek? That afternoon I had read something about the divine in a book about Plato, about how the Greeks, in moments of terrifying catastrophe or delirious joy, those moments when everything about our lives becomes dazzlingly visible in a light of almost unbearable intensity, would have an experience of the divine, the uncontrollable supreme power, which they would then refer to as "the god" or "a god," in the singular. But they were not referring to our God, the one with the capital letter. If it is about love, it is Aphrodite; if it has to do with battle and war, it is Ares. It is the god who appears in their lives, an opening to the inexplicable, which, without him or her, is too powerful, too much for us. My own life unfolds without gods, you are the only one to whom I write, perhaps that is what my questions have been about. On my travels I have encountered many forms of the divine, the gods of the Maya, the Aztecs, of the Dogon, of the Hindus. I have seen gods with a thousand arms, with a horse's head, dancing gods, flying gods, gods in animal form. I have seen you with your trident. Some gods are still feared and worshipped, others languish in books and museums; as I have said before, they can still rely on their beauty, but no longer on their power. Where did the problem begin for you Olympians? With Socrates, who, by constantly thinking aloud, began the process of removing magic from the world, even though he believed in the immortality of the soul? Or was it earlier, with Xenophanes, who accused Hesiod and Homer of having given the gods all manner of negative human habits—adultery, jealousy, deceit—and thereby damaging the notion of the divine? Did you ever devote any attention to such thoughts? In other words, did you read about how science made you disappear? Or about philosophy, with its logical proofs that denied your existence? Of course, that means my writing a letter to you is a paradox, because the letter assumes you still exist, but please allow me my questions. Did you also read about the god who superseded you all? The One God, who was not quite One enough, and in a peculiar manoeuvre became three, one of which went on to become human for thirty-three years, while still remaining God? No-one can explain in words how this is possible, says the medieval mystic Heinrich Seuse, also known as the Blessed Henry Suso, but he attempts to do so anyway, using the words of Augustine, who says that the Father already carried within him the origin of all the divinity of the son and the spirit, or the even more unfathomable statement of Thomas Aquinas, who wrote that God, in His luminous awareness, gazes upon His own Self while bending down towards His divine existence, an almost narcissistic twist. Language here is transformed, folded and stretched into an unprovable statement for which of course no mathematical formula can ever exist. Does anything about such thoughts sound familiar to you? After all, you too had a human body, but it was immortal, while the other god's was not; he was murdered on a cross. That cannot happen to you. I know you will not write back to me, but if it is true that you are immortal, perhaps you are still out there somewhere, neglected, forgotten. Sometimes, when I am far from the sea that embraces this island on all sides, and somewhere out there in the turmoil of the world, in a big city, under a bridge, I see a tramp lying beneath a piece of cardboard with just his scruffy, grizzled beard poking out, then for a very brief moment I think, blasphemously, that it is you. But even then I do not dare to approach you with all my questions.

WAR

2011. A woman in the Netherlands receives a letter from the commander of the naval forces, confirming that the wreck of the *K XVI*, hit near Borneo by a Japanese torpedo in 1941, has been found. Her father, Wim Blom, was one of the officers on board. At last she knows for certain how and where her father died. Her name is Katja Boonstra, and she is on the committee of a Dutch organisation that supports the dependants of missing WWII submarine crew members. That war will not be over until the last person connected to it is no longer alive. She discusses the news with a friend, whose father died on the same vessel. The friend tells her that she read the letter out loud to her father's photograph. Image: an elderly woman in a quiet Dutch room reading a letter to the black-and-white photograph of a dead man in a naval uniform. The world as an endless series of phenomena.

1935. A long and narrow vessel, clearly a submarine, is anchored in calm water close to the shore. I can tell it is the tropics by the trees behind the harbour buildings and the white uniforms of the crew lined up on deck, officers and sailors.

It is the arrival of Her Majesty's *K XVI* in the Dutch East Indies. Six years later, the submarine will be deployed to hunt Japanese cruisers and destroyers off the coast of Borneo, whose mission is to capture the local oilfields. Together with the *K XIV* and the *K XV*, it shadows the enemy ships, which are travelling in convoy with ten freighters. On Christmas Eve, they strike lucky. The *K XVI* follows the destroyer *Sagiri* and sinks it. Then she goes after the *Murakumo*, which gets away. A day later, Christmas 1941, a Japanese submarine, the *I-166*, sees a Dutch sub above it, and fires. The *K XVI* sinks; all lives are lost. Soon after, the *I-166* suffers the same fate and is sunk by a British submarine. The captain of that vessel is a man named Bill King.

A Dutch submarine torpedoed a Japanese ship; a Japanese submarine destroyed a Dutch one, and was then sunk by a British sub. War.

2011. A fisherman in Borneo tells some Australian divers that he knows of a wreck sixty miles off the coast. They go looking for it and find the *K XVI* forty metres down.

2003. A Japanese man lays a bouquet at the monument of the submarine fleet at the Dutch naval port of Den Helder. He is the son of one of the *I-166*'s crew and wishes to express his remorse about what his father had to do during the war. Katja Boonstra hears about it. She invites the Japanese man for a meal, and later they travel together to Ireland, to the estate of Bill King, the British captain of the submarine that torpedoed the *I-166*, and they plant a tree together. I look once again at that photograph from 1935, the slim boat, the line of men in white. One of those men is Wim Blom; his daughter cannot tell him apart from all of those other white ghosts, because of the distance from which the photograph was taken. And the sea has no eyes and can see nothing. Only the imagination can see. Two submarines deep beneath the surface, the deadly, elongated metal object leaving one vessel and boring into the other. The slow journey down, the languid pitching and tossing, death.

RATÓN

A bull always has his weapons with him. They are sharp and they are symmetrical; they make him easy to recognise. If the enemy positions himself carefully within that symmetry, not much can happen to him. But the paradox of the bullfight consists in doing just the opposite. Being gored must always remain a possibility, and great skill is required. This is a ballet with death, one that is usually won by the dancer, who must move with great elegance in the proximity of death, yet the one who must die is the bull. Sometimes that is not the outcome. All manner of barbaric festivals still take place in the Spanish provinces, with entire villages challenging bulls, running alongside them, racing ahead of them, to defy that dark danger just once; even though the tips of the horns are sometimes sawn off, an animal that weighs hundreds of kilos still has formidable power, and it is all about measuring oneself against that snorting atavism, imitating the fight with the myth, medieval rituals that usually end in grinding exhaustion, scenes of horror, drunkenness, blood, dust or mud; a few tempting fate, others revelling in provoking and screaming and in the idea that "might is right," until the other proves mightier, the animal, the emblem of the myth, emerging from the texts of antiquity as a sudden reality, and then returning to myth, a Minotaur demanding sacrifices. That happened this year, and the myth already has a name: Ratón, Mouse, a name as an antithesis, a denial, to defuse the danger. Animals should not have names, they are called what they are. As a mouse, this Mouse could not have killed people, but as a bull he could, and so he was named after a different animal, one infinitely lower in the hierarchy of emblems; there are no mice on coats of arms. He can race, chase after the men who are running ahead of him, who are dancing and capering, slapping his massive body. Five hundred kilos, a triangular patch of white right between his horns, three deaths to his name, and so his presence has become indispensable, his price has increased fivefold, death runs with him.

POSIDONIA

Can seaweed also be a memento mori? One of the beaches on the north coast of this island, a fair hike from a small fishing village, is called Cala des Tamarells. First you have to walk across a long beach that separates the sea from a freshwater area known as *albufera* in Spanish, a paradise for waterbirds, the Albufera des Grau. With the autumn rains, the water levels rise, and where the freshwater flows into the sea a narrow wooden bridge passes over a kind of stream that grows wider and wider once summer is over. The walk involves climbing and descending, Mediterranean vegetation grows all around as you climb up off the beach: wild rosemary, heather, socarrell, bruc, marram grass, and my favourite, *Euphorbia*, which now, in September, has the first green leaves on the tips of its upright brown twigs. At the top of the climb, the view changes dramatically. You can no longer see the way you have come; the path through the rocks, the village itself and the bay, with its small and larger boats at anchor, have all been left far behind, and you can see the tumble-down watchtower in the distance on its high and rocky hill. These watchtowers stand in a circle all around the island; once they were occupied.

I love that tower. It is damaged; large square blocks have fallen from the walls, and it is the only one not to have been restored. The north wind eats away at the stones, which are the same colour as the hill; whoever built it did not have to go far to hew them to make a tower in that remote place. Its isolation was probably its downfall—it is too far to transport workers, material and machines. A pair of kestrels are nesting in its cavities; when I am there I sometimes hear them screeching, high and shrill. At the foot of the hill is a small beach that is never cleaned, covered with dead seaweed that washes ashore and piles up, enormous pillows and mattresses of dead vegetation, a love bed for giants. Gulls, kestrels, seaweed, sometimes a fishing boat that does not come too close to the shore before veering away again, a small island across the water, where no-one lives. When the weather becomes wild, which happens quite frequently, the sea whips walls of foam high up onto the rocks. At moments like this I would like to be under the water, watching the Posidonia, the meadows of tall, green, supple seaweed that I swim through on calmer days. Luxuriant—that is the right word, the long, narrow leaves so vibrantly green, dancing gently with the movement of the water; they are, in the most literal sense, water plants, Poseidon's grass, *Posidonia oceanica*. I called it seaweed, but it is in fact just a plant with roots, leaves and a stem, which provides food and shelter for fish and small crustaceans and loses its leaves when the winter storms come, which the tide then deposits on the beach, piling them up in layer upon layer. They turn brown, those long leaves, their damp woody colour taking on a silver gleam, a layer of gradual decay protecting the coast, a huge bed made of millions of leaves. As you walk over it, it bounces gently. The swaying green of down below has lost its lustre, it has something to say about decay and death, but when the wind lifts it up and chases it to the sandy slope beyond the beach, it brings organic matter blowing along with it to feed the plants on the land and on the hill. Meanwhile, beneath the water, the rot continues in a more frivolous way, as the beds of Posidonia are full of decomposing fibres that are torn away and wash up on the coast, where the waves beat across the beach, sculpting them into small, brown, furry balls, which the islanders call *pets de monja*, nuns' farts.

There is nothing in this letter that the god does not know, but perhaps the nuns' farts would amuse him, because even a god has never held a fart in his hand. They feel hairy in your hand, his sea is an artist that can transform dead material into a new form, camel-coloured, with the smallest sparkle of fibres that once danced in his gardens, swaying to the rhythm of his eternal music.

POSEIDON XXI

Do gods read? I mean no disrespect, but it suddenly occurred to me that I could not think of a single image of a god reading. Now that may not count for much, as my memory is growing worse, but the question came to me via two entirely different routes. The first time was when I was reading what a modern physicist had to say about Thales of Miletus' notion that water was the originating material of everything. The author then goes on to deal with them one by one, all those amazing early thinkers who went in search of the substance of which all other things are supposedly a transitory form. Unlike his teacher Thales, Anaximander believed that it could not be water or any other substance; it had to be something that was ageless, infinite and eternal, something containing the entire known world, a great chain of being and becoming, an ongoing struggle of winning and losing, victory and defeat, a war constantly declared anew, of hot against cold, dry against wet, fire against water, with an ultimate reconciliation over time, also repeated over and over again, endless series of worlds appearing and disappearing. Did you gods read anything about this? Did such ideas concern you too? Or were you blissfully wrapped up in your own myths, certain of worship and sacrifices, sure of your ground? Those men, living in Miletus or Sicily, all wanted to know: Empedocles with his four elements, Heraclitus with his idea of Change as an ever-present principle, but they could not prove what they thought and claimed, they lived on conjecture and intuition, the Void, the Fire, the beautifully ordered cosmos, the eternal and indestructible atoms of Democritus and Leucippus. Surely all that must have interested you Olympians? Or did you already resent the doubt, the constant questioning of mortals who might one day dream up an idea that would mean your end?

And the second time? That is of an entirely different order of magnitude. At the back of my Hesiod, there are *Testimonia*, accounts written about him by contemporaries and those who came later. But before I move on to that, what did you think of Hesiod? Did you read him? And Homer? Most people like to read what others write about them. Does this also apply to gods? Quintilian is reticent. He feels that my beloved Hesiod "takes flight only rarely, and much of his work is filled with proper names, but his didactic maxims are useful, and the smoothness of his choice and arrangement of words can be recommended: he wins the palm in the middle style." Sparing in his praise, a true critic. You may not have read Aristotle either, not even when he was writing about nectar and ambrosia, the food of the gods, your daily bread. How would you have responded if you had read it? "For if they (i.e. the gods) take hold of nectar and ambrosia for the sake of pleasure, then these are not at all the cause of their being; but if it is for the sake of being, how can they be eternal if they are in need of nourishment? But about mythic sophistries it is not worth inquiring seriously." A stern teacher.

No, the nightmarish vision that prompted my question about your reading is of a different kind. It comes from a book by Diogenes Laertius, *Lives of Eminent Philosophers*. In that book, Hieronymus of Rhodes says that when Pythagoras descended into the underworld, he saw Hesiod's screaming soul bound to a bronze pillar and Homer's soul suspended from a tree, with snakes surrounding it, as a punishment for all the things they had said about the gods. So there is the proof that you gods had read both Hesiod and Homer, and had called in your brother Hades to exact this terrible punishment. It is the ultimate in censorship. And it happened even though we know that all of the tales about your scandalous lives are true. These are not the lives of saints. Adultery, revenge, lust, betrayal on the battlefield, rape, patricide, perhaps that is why you remain immortal, because of the genius of the poets' writings, and what they tell us about you even today.

OLD

Do you know this living fossil? I stepped out of the metro station next to the botanical garden and saw the big fish, read the question on the poster. No, I do not know that fish. The sign is large, and so is the fish. Its mouth seems to be slightly upturned, the left eye gleams blackly, on the look-out. If this fish were to speak, it would be to issue a threat. It has been living in our planet's waters for twenty-three million years, says the poster, and that too sounds like a threat. I look at the photograph. That lurking head is followed by the huge body; later I learn that it can grow to four and a half metres in length and weigh two hundred kilos. Pirarucú, *Arapaima gigas*. Place of residence: here, the Amazon. This is our privilege, the ability to see worlds that were always hidden from humankind. Medellín's aquarium is near the botanical garden; on this weekday it is very quiet there. Doubly quiet: the absence of other people, and the silence of the fish in their soundless world. I do not know if there is any correlation between silence and colour, but the intensity of the colours is inversely proportional to the silence in the transparent water behind the glass walls. It is hard to grasp that these are living creatures, as they sometimes hang there in their element for so long without moving, yellow, purple, striped, knifefish, piranhas, murderers, meditating monks, deadly weapons and pacifists, medusas made of transparent jelly, anemones that look like intestines with gently swaying protuberances, raised fingers, future corals the colour of blood. I walk past the silently bowing courtiers to the place where Pirarucú lives. He has the largest house, which he shares with a few other languid residents, who do not resemble him. I see a tree with roots suspended in the water. Here we are in his imitation world, I can look up at the surface of the water from beneath, a mysteriously moving membrane that I will later see from above, but not yet. What does it mean if a fish is twenty-three million years old? To put it another way, this fish is not twenty-three million years old, so why do I believe that it is? Animals are repeated versions of themselves; three thousand or thirty thousand years before Christ, Pirarucú looked just the same, and why do I think that this fish, swimming extremely slowly back and forth, right in front of me, knows that? He is from before Cheops, before Gilgamesh, before Homer, before Poseidon, before everything that we latecomers call old. He is from a different mythology. The Uaiás tribe knows his tale: he was a warrior punished by the gods, who smote him with a bolt of lightning straight through the heart. While he was still alive, they threw him into the depths of the river, where he changed into a fish with large scales. The brooding eye peers at me every time he passes, but can he really see me too? Or am I not worth the effort, a ghost from a non-existent world? When I go up to the next floor, I see the water from above, and his dark shadow moving to and fro. The tree whose roots I saw down below rises high above the water now, the green of its leaves bringing me back to my own world. The surface of the water, that incredibly fine division between above and below, has a different function here, closing off the silent universe beneath, locking away the mystery, prohibiting access with its gentle movement. I am shut out, I am only a human being, I do not belong there. Later, in a village on the Brazilian Amazon, I will eat him, and it will feel like sacrilege. Him? Her? I know she lays her eggs in a nest on the bottom of the great river and looks after them until the young hatch, after which they are incubated inside the father's mouth. Why does that too feel like some strange religion? As I walk away and into the botanical garden, I think of questions for another letter to the sea god. Is he also in charge of rivers? Of rivers like this one, which are as big as a sea? Does he know the gods who punished Pirarucú? And the most difficult question of all: how old is he himself? But I know that I will receive no answer.

FLAME

It is one of the more peculiar moments in Dante's Hell, where everything is already so cruel and strange. Dante is in a pensive mood. He wonders "if near morning our dreams are true." The Dutch version that I am reading alongside the Italian is an old-fashioned literal translation from 1940, clumsy and awkward in places, and therefore effective in a peculiar way, as if the dust of seventy years that lies over the words and the sentences were a symbol of the antiquity of the text itself. We are in the 26th Canto of the *Inferno*, in the place of punishment reserved for false counsellors. Dante is travelling with his guide and teacher Virgil, and they are reflecting on the forbidden, by means of an apocryphal story about a final journey of Odysseus once told by Pliny, a wild fantasy in which Odysseus, whom Dante calls Ulisse, travels beyond the boundaries of the known world, never to return. In doing so, he violates one of God's commandments.

I once stood on the western tip of the island of Hierro, the westernmost of the Canary Islands. Nature and humans had conspired: the sun was setting dramatically, a cross stood on the last rock and on one of the arms of the cross sat a raven who, like me, was silently looking out over the endless sea, which was awash with red, a warning. The medieval traveller could not go beyond this point, it was forbidden by God himself, and anyone who insisted on doing so would fall off the world and disappear into nothingness.

Less than two centuries after Dante, Columbus set off from precisely this point; belief had turned into superstition, something you could sail through to reach a new world, just as philosophy and astronomy had entered new territory, with the risk of becoming bogged down in the marshes of heresy, and the punishment of being burned at the stake for Giordano Bruno and humiliating silence for Galileo, forced to bite his tongue, even though he was right.

I do not know if Columbus had read Dante and so knew how the world had once looked to the poet and his contemporaries: a quarter inhabited, the land in the east bounded by the Ganges, in the southern hemisphere and half of the northern hemisphere only sea, and, in the poet's imagination, within the immeasurable waters of the southern hemisphere, the steep mountain of Purgatory opposite heavenly Jerusalem. In Dante's account this is where Odysseus came to grief, because human beings were not permitted to see that mountain. But the poet does not tell the story himself, he pulls Odysseus from his eternal box of poetic tricks. As he follows "the lonely way among the rocks and splinters of the ridge" with his teacher Virgil, he comes across a sea of flames burning in the eighth ditch, "so each flame moves along the gullet of the ditch, for none shows the theft and every one steals away a sinner." When they come closer, they can see the individual flames. One of these flames has a peculiar shape and the one poet asks the other, his guide in the underworld, who "is in that fire which comes so cloven at the top," and his master responds: "Within there are tormented Ulysses and Diomed." Dante, who knew Homer, having already encountered him on this dark journey, but who had perhaps not read all of his works, wants to hear what that "horned flame" has to say, and Virgil advises him not to speak to the Greek heroes himself. Ulysses and Diomedes are powerful men, he says, who might look down on Dante or disdain his foreign tongue. So the teacher does the talking and an answer is forthcoming.

"The greater horn of the ancient flame began to toss and murmur just as if it were being beaten by the wind." When you read this, you need to take a step back and imagine yourself there as a third person, otherwise you are not reading it correctly. Two men are standing on a rocky path in hell, talking to a flame, and that flame tells them that he set out with his old and slow companions "with but one ship and with that little company which had not deserted me" and sailed through "that narrow outlet where Hercules set up his landmarks so that men should not pass beyond" and past Morocco, heading for the unpeopled world.

His crew paid dearly for their attempt. For a while, it seemed as though they would make it. They could already see the stars of the other pole, and the forbidden mountain, dim in the distance, higher than any mountain Ulisse had ever seen before, but then "a storm rose and struck the forepart of the ship. Three times it whirled her round with all the waters, the fourth time lifted the poop aloft and plunged the prow below, as One willed, until the sea closed again over us."

The "One" has no capital letter in Dante's Italian. But this time it was not Poseidon who, in his need for revenge, did not want Odysseus=Ulysses=Ulisse ever to return home to Penelope, but the vengeful God Himself, the God of before and after, who, according to Dante, caused Odysseus to drown in Poseidon's sea, destroying Homer's masterpiece at one stroke by changing the ending so barbarically.

POSEIDON XXII

The puzzles do not end. I have a condition that I call tumbling thoughts, a state of confusion that sends me spinning from one thought to another. It is autumn, the fig tree outside my studio has lost its leaves, just a few large ones still hang near its base. It is a day without wind, so when I see them moving I know the tortoise is there, not the big one, but the little one, whom I recognise by his markings. He is a member of the nobility, he bears his own coat of arms. He knows me too and has decided I am harmless, even though I am trespassing on his property. As soon as I see him, the thoughts begin to tumble, and I walk over to him. He raises his old philosopher's head and, looking up into the sun, tries to gauge my size. He does not seem disappointed, I recognise that expression on his face, a form of satisfaction linked to the fact that Achilles has once again been unable to catch up with him. And then another tumble and I am with Achilles, and of course that takes me back to you, and the disgraceful way you behaved on the battlefield at Troy. But I stick with Achilles, which takes me to the King of Spain, who has had an operation on his Achilles tendon. I often see the old Bourbon hobbling

along, and the sympathy I feel should be taken in its most
literal sense, as I too suffer with my Achilles tendon. I
occasionally feel an excruciating pain in the spot where the
immortal Thetis held her mortal son when she dipped him
into the water to make him invulner-able; somehow you
remain our eternal point of reference. But now the tumbling really starts, because if you were a church, Achilles
would number among my saints and divinities, alongside
Odysseus and Athene and Aphrodite and Orion and Pro-
metheus. You might be surprised that I have not named
you, even though I am writing to you, not to the others.
It surprises me too; that is what I meant about puzzles.
The only answer I can think of is that it must be to do
with the sea, that incredible attraction mixed with fear
that oceans have exerted on me ever since the first time,
when, still a young man, I sailed to South America on
a small ship. It was a crew of fourteen men and a small
boat makes it easier to appreciate the infinity of the sea
and to feel it tugging at the vessel; at night, when you
stand alone on deck and gaze out into the darkness at the
undulating, shifting water, our own existence turns into an
endless question without answer—it must be something
along those lines. Later, I visited your empty temples on
Cape Sounion and at Segesta on Sicily, classical husks of
great beauty, mighty Doric columns with the heavens for a
roof, where the imagination transforms the sound of trees
into human voices that perhaps still speak about you, but
perhaps not. And here, where I am now, I have the sea, and
therefore you, around me at all times. Has this brought me
closer to you? I do not believe so, but still I look out for
you. The more I read, the more forms you assume, most of
them unpleasant. Conflict with Athene and Hera, always

a tsunami to hand if something displeased you, an expert in destruction. Is that the attraction? The same feeling I experience when the sea here rages, lashing metres of furious foam against the rocks. At times like that, when I see a boat sailing in the distance, struggling to reach a harbour, then I think of Odysseus, cunning and mortal, who for all your divine power always keeps one step ahead of you. He is one of my saints for that reason alone. Does that make you jealous? I know, he had murdered one of your many sons, who would have killed him otherwise, but must your revenge last eternally? As Homer wrote an account of it, I am allowed to be present when the gods convene and Athene pleads with Zeus on behalf of Odysseus, who is held captive in the dark caves of Calypso and still cannot return home, unlike the other survivors of the war, because this daughter of Atlas has enchanted him and is trying to make the man forget the island, while he dreams of seeing something of Ithaca, anything at all, even if only the smoke of a fire, and he wishes only to die if he cannot return. I hear her father's answer: that he has not forgotten the god-like but mortal Odysseus, but that you, Poseidon, begrudge him his death and want to force him to journey ever onwards, an eternal exile. We know how it ended: you did not succeed. But the mystery of your fury remains, returning with every winter storm.

A statue of you was found off Cape Artemision, bronze, slightly taller than a man. Your naked body faces us, but the statue appears to be standing sideways, because your head is turned to the left and your eyes are following the direction of your left arm, which is also pointing in a straight line to the left in an almost pacifying gesture, as though intended to calm the fury of the sea. It is a statue of immense power, yet the right hand is not outstretched like the left one, but lifted slightly higher in the empty air, the fingers making an elegant, almost feminine gesture. Is that the secret?

COLLEAGUES

A foetal cow's head, pinky white, no eyes, horns made of the same smooth, plastic-like material. Where there should be an eye, there is no more than a dark shadow; beneath that, where we might expect a shoulder, there is a single eye. A voluminous ball gown, also pink, floating airily over a few thick lines which, when they emerge from beneath the transparent skirt, turn out to be tentacles. She is dancing alone in the most austere of ballrooms, the movement lending her an air of infinite lightness and grace. The walls of the ballroom are the black of the deepest ocean, the light illuminating her as she whirls through the darkness must come from the camera depicting her in her lightless world, an octopus of great beauty.

Stauroteuthis syrtensis. She does not know it, but that is her name. Two and a half kilometres beneath the waves, where no light penetrates—that is where she lives. If she wishes to go somewhere, she uses her fins, which resemble the ears of an elephant. Or she starts pumping water in and out through her mantle, propelling herself through the overwhelming silence. We are not like her, but what we have in common is that we exist and that we need to eat. We do not know how she would describe us.

Two buttocks of taut pig's bladder, and between them an elegant double vulva that is not a vulva, the skin bluish with the shadow of a pink embryo that is not an embryo. Perfect curves, but otherwise no familiar points of reference. *Chaetopterus pugaporcinus*, the pigbutt worm. She too moves through the inky black void without making a sound. She feeds herself by inflating a bubble of mucus that collects organic particles on its surface. I look again at the perfect bluish orbs of those two balloons, the white haze of fleeting dots, the wondrous symmetrical pink folds of a woman but with no woman there. Nothing here is as it seems, but she too must eat to live.

Such unimaginable gluttony in just twenty centimetres of fish that consists almost entirely of head. A crumpled, badly folded blue bag of poorly sewn material with that head on top, a wicked protuberance below, the maw open to the lightless black that knows neither shade nor nuance, the teeth white and sharp like inwardly pointing daggers, another dagger with a luminous tip between those glowing blue eyes. This too is a female. *Melanocetus johnsonii*. She does not like movement, and so her enemies cannot find her. Their ghostly little male companions remain with them for a lifetime, before gradually dissolving into the tissues of the female body, until nothing of them remains—this is a story with a moral. The black sea-devil, or humpback anglerfish, dwells between one hundred and four thousand metres below sea level. Down there, as the French biologist Monod said, it is cold, it is dark, it is deep, it is hungry. Jaws, tentacles, fans of arrows, wings with teeth, membranes with ivory hooks, camouflaged or transparent; down in the icy coldness, the pandemonium of Hieronymus Bosch, the court of the sea god, waits, hunts, eats. This god did not make them—and yet he must know them all.

STONE

The attraction of some objects, particularly when they have no objective value whatsoever, is sometimes impossible to explain. We are talking about something that, for the sake of convenience, I call a stone, even though it is not one. And yet if I were to throw my stone, which is not a stone, at someone and it were to hit him, he would surely maintain that I had thrown a stone at him.

It was a rainy afternoon in Buenos Aires. I had heard that there was a nature park not far from the city centre, along the banks of the River Plate. A sign at the gate said the park was closed, but the gate itself was slightly open and so I went in. Suddenly the city was far away, and I was walking through a lagoon-like area, with brownish plants disguised as dead reeds looming up from dark water. For some time I saw no-one, but after half an hour I spotted a man in a rain cape sitting on a bench beneath a tree. I asked him where the river was, and he showed me the way, a wide path full of stones the colour of mud. I had once stood in a graveyard in Montevideo over on the other side of the river, which is so broad and expansive at this point that the opposite bank is invisible, and had thought about the people who had been thrown out of aeroplanes there during the dictatorship. No sign of that was visible, and yet it was there. Absent, present. Perhaps that was why I felt the need to visit the river this time, as it is a river that, with its vast emptiness, has something of the sea about it. It started to rain harder, and so my walk began to feel like a spiritual exercise, something to be endured, but that would conclude with a reward: a panorama. It was quiet, the beat of my feet a clock without numbers. I saw brown birds whose names I did not know; clouds the colour of zinc and lead sailed above as if they were travelling along with me, and together we arrived at the river, which was as wide as I had hoped and spoke of how far it had come. A slope where the water had deposited all kinds of objects: branches, tree stumps, a dead fish, empty plastic bottles, stones. And my stone. I saw it immediately because of its redness, but it was not only red. It was more like the petrified banner of an unknown regiment: red, light grey, red. I picked it up and it lay there in my hand, small and light. The rain had stopped for a moment, a pool of light appeared among the clouds like a hole in the ice, the stone, still wet, gleamed gently. Now I could see it better and understand how the river had shaped it. The red was terracotta, baked earth, the red of two bricks sealed together with cement, which had once tumbled into the water as part of a wall, slowly wearing away, and now chosen by me as a travelling companion.

My stone is here now, where I am writing this, in Spain. Worthless, insignificant, necessary. I use stones and shells to make spaces my own. I cannot express it any other way. An anonymous hotel room becomes my room because of a shell or a stone I have selected for that purpose. An amulet, a fetish that must satisfy two conditions: it must be insignificant and worthless to other people, and yet have a beauty that those others cannot perceive. I take the stone in my hand, it feels dry and cool. Our relationship is one of exemplary loyalty. When I am writing, my stone sits beside me. Today I am leaving on my travels, and when I return in a few weeks my stone will be there. I do not know if it remembers the house to which it once belonged. All I know is that it lay there, wet and red, on a day with lots of rain, beside a wide river that was on its way to the ocean.

POSEIDON XXIII

This is to be the final letter. It is winter on the island, and when I go outside I feel the cold wind coming from the sea. Big cloud-ships sail by, already rigged out in the colour of the night. Wind moves the wild olive trees around the house. These trees are called Elaios in the ancient Greek of Rhodes, they were meant to keep evil spirits away from human beings. The neighbours' donkey is denouncing the world. This is the hour of the owl and the curlew, when everything that has no words still wishes to say something. Over the past few years I have occupied myself with the fiction that is you, because what are gods but dreams, figments of the imagination, answers to the questions without answers of which we are made? We have given you attributes so that we can recognise you; you had to look like us so we too would become part of the fiction. We have participated in the game, sacrificed, prayed, we have wondered if we are also a fiction to you, a shadow and reflection in our eternal game of arrival and departure, of florescence and destruction, we who change just as little as you. If you have laughed at me, I can accept that; I know my place. You and your fellow gods are from an age before writing, symbols of a world before history, when women still had power, when they chose kings for their bed, who would be killed after a year of service that passed all too quickly, thrown from the rocks into the sea or torn to pieces. Mass migrations echo through your stories, the struggle for hegemony, between regions and islands, between women and men. You gods came from the east in constantly changing forms, always shifting to reflect the image of people who were there before you and who invented you so that they might understand the world, until the moment came when we realised it was all a dream, a poem that had seemed to be about you and your fellow gods, but was in fact only about us all along. When you said nothing more, we went on asking questions, finding thousands and thousands of answers, about the smallest and the largest things, about the visible and the invisible; soon we will travel to the planets that bear your names, because we still seek the answer that continues to elude us. Sometimes, in the grip of nostalgia, we look at your statues, the images of our desire for power and immortality, for protection in the vast, empty, floorless halls of the universe.

You have never answered me, but that was not necessary. When I stand beside the sea, I can hear you with your thousand voices. Sometimes you scream, uproarious laughter that mocks every question, on other nights you are as still as death, a mirror in which the stars can see themselves. At such times, I think that you might wish to say something to me, but you never do. Of course I know that I have been sending letters to nobody. But what if, tomorrow, out on the rocks, I should happen to find a trident?

San Luis, July 2008
Hofgut Missen, June 2012

NOTES AND ILLUSTRATIONS

Fig. 1

POSEIDON I

Fig. 2: The twelve Olympian gods, depicted in a relief said to be from Tarentum (1st century B.C.–1st century A.D.)

MARRIED TO A HAT

La Dépêche, July 25, 2008

SIEGE

Pieter Snayers (1592–1667), a Flemish painter who studied under Sebastiaen Vrancx and is known for his fantastic battle scenes, painted with a great eye for detail, magnificent depictions, in which the topographical details are correct. His repertoire also included smaller military drawings, paintings of mounted battles and hunting scenes.

Fig. 3: Pieter Snayers, *Troops at the Siege of Aire-sur-la-Lys*, 1653, Museo Nacional del Prado, Madrid

INVALIDES

Fig. 4: *Le Monde*, August 21, 2008, online article about a funeral ceremony for French soldiers who had died in Afghanistan.

POSEIDON III

"Poseidon" in Franz Kafka, *Beschreibung eines Kampfes. Novellen, Skizzen, Aphorismen aus dem Nachlaß*, Fischer Verlag, Frankfurt am Main, 1989

RIVER

Fig. 5

CHALLENGER

Fig. 6

POSEIDON IV

Un punto solo m'è maggior letargo
che venticinque secoli alla 'mpresa
che fè Nettuno ammirar l'ombra d'Argo.

"A single moment makes for me deeper oblivion than
five and twenty centuries upon the enterprise that made
Neptune wonder at the shadow of the Argo."

Dante, *Paradiso*, Canto XXXIII, 94–96

Dante Alighieri, *The Divine Comedy*, Italian text with translation
and comment by John D. Sinclair, Oxford University Press, 1939

Fig. 7: Lindau, market square

ASCLEPIAS

François-René de Chateaubriand, *Mémoires d'outre-tombe*, Classiques Garnier Multimédia, Collection "Classiques Garnier," Paris, 1998

LORRY

Fig. 8

The article appeared in *The Times* on August 31, 2009. Subsequent reports in other newspapers gave a different account of events, but the mystery remains.

KENKŌ

Yoshida Kenkō (born c. 1283–died c. 1350; it must be wonderful to have been born, and to have died, circa—"around"—a date, allowing one to float in time a little) was a courtier, poet and monk, an irresistible combination. He gave up his position at the court in Kyoto, in those days known as Heian, following the death of Emperor Go-Uda, and entered a Buddhist monastery. Such a course of events was apparently more common in Japan than in Europe. The famous *Tale*

Fig. 9

of Genji, written just after the year 1000, is full of aristocratic men and women who withdrew to a monastery, sometimes long before their lives came to an end. Kenkō's *Tsurezuregusa*, a collection of prose pieces, is one of the classics of Japanese literature. The book consists of 243 pieces and meditations, most of them short or very short, about transience, death and the pleasure of solitude.

The illustration on the cover is by Nishikawa Sukenobu (1671–1751), a master of *ukiyo-e* (the "floating world"), the coloured woodcuts that were so popular in Japan from the seventeenth to the twentieth century, and which are still highly sought-after collector's items. His speciality was woodcuts, drawings and paintings of artists, and of women from a wide range of backgrounds. Two artists collaborating across a gulf of many centuries: a constant source of wonder.

Essays in Idleness, The Tsurezuregusa of Kenkō, translated by Donald Keene, Charles E. Tuttle Co. Publishers, Tokyo, 1981/1997

POSEIDON VI

Some years ago, I attended a concert at Carnegie Hall of music by one of my favourite composers, Elliott Carter, who was about to turn one hundred. This doyen of modern American classical music died in November 2012, at the age of 103.

In 1950, inspired by Igor Stravinsky and Charles Ives, he lived for a year in the desert of Arizona, in order to free himself from neoclassicism and to find his own musical idiom, which was more brusque and complex than his earlier work, and did not shy away from disson-ance. He wrote his first opera, *What Next?*, when he was almost ninety.

"Scrivo in Vento" (I write in the wind) is a composition for flute, dedicated to the flautist Robert Aitken. The piece was played for the first time in Avignon in 1991. Its title comes from a sonnet by Petrarch, who lived in and around Avignon for many years.

INFANTICIDE

From an article in the *Schwäbische Zeitung* (January 11, 2011). The murderer was 25-year-old Miloslav Maletic, who was known to the police. "The six-year-old brother of the victim probably had to witness his brother being beaten to death."

BOOKS

Fig.10: Photograph by Max Mettler, published in Roman
Signer, *Bücher*, Gebrüder König Postkartenverlag, Köln, 1984

POSEIDON VII

Fig. 11: Francisco de Goya, *Saturno devorando a un hijo* (Saturn Devouring His Son), 1820–1823, Museo Nacional del Prado, Madrid

WALL

Fig. 12

BLUR

Ingmar Bergman's 1963 film *Nattvardsgästerna* (literally, The Communicants) is generally known as *Winter Light* in English.

POSEIDON VIII

Pascal was familiar with the notion of God as a sphere; anyone who wishes to know more may read Borges, who goes into detail about Pascal's sphere in his essay "La esfera de Pascal" in *Otras Inquisiciones*, translated by Ruth Simms as *Other Inquisitions, 1937–1952*, University of Texas Press, 1975.

HÖLDERLIN

Fig. 13: Friedrich Hölderlin, pencil drawing (1823)
by Rudolf Lohbauer and Johann Georg Schreiner, with a note by Eduard Mörike.

The line is from Friedrich Hölderlin's poem "Der Sommer," in
Sämtliche Werke in sechs Bänden, Vol. II, published by Friedrich
Beißner, Cotta, Stuttgart 1953.

PAINTING

Adriaen Brouwer (1605–1638), Flemish painter, influenced by
Pieter Bruegel and Frans Hals, as can be seen from the way Brouwer painted people fighting in the tavern (Bruegel) and his incredibly
skilful use of light and the contrast between dark earthy colours and
shades of grey (Hals). Later in his brief life, he focused on landscapes

Fig. 14: Peter Paul Rubens, *Neptune and Amphitrite, c.* 1615, Gemäldegalerie der Staatlichen Museen zu Berlin. The painting has been missing since the Second World War.

at dusk and in soft moonlight, in which human beings appear to be at the mercy of a hostile, sometimes malevolent nature. It is not surprising that he was one of Beckett's favourite painters. Some of Beckett's plays would have perfectly suited such a landscape, just as those landscapes could have been situated in Beckett's own homeland.

Erika Tophoven, *Becketts Berlin*, Nicolaische Verlagsbuchhandlung, Berlin, 2005

Fig. 15: Adriaen Brouwer, *Landscape with Bowlers*, 1635–1637, Gemäldegalerie der Staatlichen Museen zu Berlin

POSEIDON IX

Cicero, *De natura deorum*, in a translation by H. Rackham, Loeb Classical Library, Harvard University Press, Cambridge, first edition 1933
Plato, *Cratylus*, in a translation by H. N. Fowler, Loeb Classical Library, Harvard University Press, Cambridge, first edition 1926

ORION

Fig. 16

PASTORALE

Written in Missen, in the deep south of Germany, amongst the forest and meadows of the Allgäu, on one of those days when it begins to thaw and the snow turns grey and disappears, giving back the soil to the sunlight and the birds.

POSEIDON X

Fig. 17: Leonardo da Vinci, *Neptune*,
c. 1504, The Royal Collection

I later discovered that Leonardo da Vinci's *Neptune* is not in fact a pencil drawing, but was done in black chalk.

Helen Scales, *Poseidon's Steed. The Story of Seahorses, from Myth to Reality*, Gotham Books/Penguin, New York, 2009

CONVERSATION

Napoleon and Talleyrand on Madame de Staël. Talleyrand owed his position as Minister of Foreign Affairs in the Directory to De Staël, but the fact that he regained the position under Napoleon, and once again under Louis XVIII, was something he owed only to his indomitable self.

Franz Blei, *Talleyrand oder der Zynismus*, Rowohlt, Berlin, 1932

AGAVE

Fig. 18

POSEIDON XI

Fig. 19: *Sbarco dal Bucintoro del doge Sebastiano Ziani al Convento della Carità*, anonymous Italian miniature, sixteenth century

WITNESS

Fig. 20: The Arab Spring of January and February 2011
also saw looting at the Egyptian Museum in Cairo

de Volkskrant, February 3, 2011

POSEIDON XII

What prompted me to write this letter was a piece by Patrick Leigh Fermor in the *Times Literary Supplement* of October 14, 1977, about Edmund Keeley's book *Cavafy's Alexandria: Study of a Myth in Progress* (Harvard University Press, 1976), in which he wrote, "The end of Athens at the battle of Chaeronea used to be the signal for Greek scholars to put back their books with a Milton quotation and a sigh." Later in the same piece, Leigh Fermor links this fatal end to later battles, but Chaeronea had already led me to Polybius, book 18, chapter 14, with the story of Demosthenes and the betrayal, and its implications for Cavafy's work.

Polybius (c. 200 to 120 B.C.), Greek historian and philosopher known particularly for his *Historíai*, an account of the period between the First Punic War and the destruction of Carthage and Corinth. In my novel *Allerzielen* (translated into English by Susan Massotty as *All Souls' Day*), I used a quote from him that I had come across somewhere. That brought me into contact with the classicist Dr Wolther Kassies, the Dutch translator of Polybius' work, which resulted not only in a most fascinating correspondence, but also, for me, in a close study of Polybius. It felt like reading a newspaper written on marble: delegations, sieges, negotiations, war, all the things we know, with one important difference, the time factor, as messages from distant regions took an endless length of time to reach the capital or to travel from there to reach the protagonists at the scene of the action, with all the uncertainty that entailed. And yet, in spite of the lengthy gaps in communication between the various parties, nothing appears to have changed in essence and Polybius remains a gripping read.

Polybius, *Histories*, translated into Dutch as *Wereldgeschiedenis* by Wolther Kassies, Athenaeum–Polak & Van Gennep, Amsterdam 2007; into English by Evelyn S. Shuckburgh, Macmillan, London/New York, 1889, reprinted Bloomington, 1962

CHAIR

Gimpo Airport, Seoul, South Korea.

DONKEYS

Fig. 21

The pleasure of strange names and unexpected events. September 2010, and I am in Seoul, breaking a journey from Beijing to Kyoto. It is afternoon, a gentle rain is falling, and although I think I am looking for the Gyeonghuigung annexe at the Seoul Museum of Art, I am actually on my way to the Palace of the Popes in Avignon. What I do know is that a Media Art Bienniale is taking place, and that I would like to go and take a look around.

I stepped out of the silent metro at Seosomun-ro, found my way to Saemunan-gil, and am now in the museum's annexe. Before I know it, I have walked into a large, silent space with a number of screens and I can hear the sound of donkeys' hoofs on the medieval stone floors of the French popes' palace. Such moments, their utter unexpectedness, are the salt of life. There are not many visitors, the sound of their footsteps is lost in the donkeys' stampede, after a while I have forgotten the dual nature of the situation—a journey within a journey. It is not until later that I read about Douglas Gordon and the how and the why of the images I have seen. Gordon is an artist from Glasgow who "manipulates the duration of scenes from well-known films in order to interrupt the consistent flow of time and subvert their narrative structure, suggesting a new mode of perception that provokes the viewer's psychological reactions." Tinkering with time, undermining plots—always a good thing.

But what I see is something else. Donkeys were considered taboo in the middle ages, they were "regarded as inauspicious animals symbolic of ignorance, indolence, and intemperance. In contrast, many folktales describe the animal as a comic and friendly character." According to the biennial's programme, the artist wished to demonstrate the ambiguity of such judgements about good and evil. I am never too concerned with what is said about a work of art and what its "intended meaning" might be. Far from home, I saw a number of endearing donkeys trotting around a palace, and for a moment it threw me, a daydream in the afternoon, and a form of transcendence.

The title of the video installation, *Travail with My Donkeys*, is of course a reference to *Travels with a Donkey in the Cévennes*, Robert Louis Stevenson's book about his journey with a donkey (in the singular).

http://trustseoul.wordpress.com/trustartists/douglas-gordon/

GARDEN

Daitoku-ji, founded in 1315 by Akamatsu Norimura for the famous Zen master Myōchō, is in the city of Kyoto. The buildings date from the sixteenth and seventeenth centuries. There is a sub-temple within the large complex, the Ryogen-in, to which this garden belongs. The complex appears to be endless, you can wander around it for hours.

POSEIDON XIII

Fig. 22

Menorca: 40 paisatjes personals, Pere Fraga Arguimbau i Francesc Xavier Roig (ed.), Institut d'Estudis Baleàrics, Mahon, 2011, pp.109–13

Duncan Ackery, *Living in the Mediterranean*; "a small land mass of limestone and Devonian rock"

Enciclopèdia de Menorca, Primer Tom/Geografia Física, Obra Cultural Balear, Mahon, 1981

BLOOD MOON

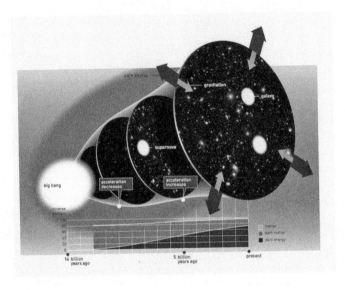

Fig. 23

I found the word "blood moon" in my 2011 garden calendar, on October 12, with the following explanation: "Full moon—according to the lunar calendar, this is the hunter's moon, or blood moon. The last of the harvest had been gathered and this was the time when the hunt began and animals were slaughtered for the winter supplies. This moon behaves in the same way as the harvest moon, hanging above the horizon shortly after sunset."

The information in my piece comes from an article in *El País* about the accelerating expansion of the universe, written by Álvaro de Rújula, "Premios Nobel de Ciencias 2011, Con galaxias y a lo loco, La aceleración de la expansión del universo" (Madrid, October 12, 2011).

"Con galaxias y a lo loco" can perhaps best be translated as "galaxies running wild"—an alarming idea for anyone who has ever seen horses stampeding.

MAN

Written in Kyoto, autumn 2010.

SURFACE

Fig. 24: *The Rescue of Saint Peter*, Egbert-Codex, *c.* 980, Reichenau, Stadtbibliothek Trier

GREEN

Fig. 25

There was a piece about Hanny's Voorwerp in the *Frankfurter Allgemeine Zeitung*, January 2011, nr. 9. In the article, the Dutch word "Voorwerp" (object) was left untranslated and, in true mythological fashion, Hanny was allocated a different gender. But her Object is what gives the depths of the cosmos its green glow. In the days that followed, there was praise from scientists all over the world, but in the Netherlands the cesspit of the internet opened wide. The rabble residing there appeared to get very hot under the collar about a woman finding something of importance. Speculation about the nature of the "object" revealed a sad lack of imagination: dildos, puns, puerility—in short, a glimpse into the worst of modern-day sleaze and slime.

POSEIDON XV

Fig. 26

ΙΛΙΑΔΟΣ Θ (viii)   107

τρὶς δ' ἄρ' ἀπ' Ἰδαίων ὀρέων κτύπε μητίετα Ζεὺς   170
cῆμα τιθεὶc Τρώεccι, μάχηc ἐτεραλκέα νίκην.
Ἕκτωρ δὲ Τρώεccιν ἐκέκλετο μακρὸν ἀύcαc·
" Τρῶεc καὶ Λύκιοι καὶ Δάρδανοι ἀγχιμαχηταί,
ἀνέρεc ἔcτε, φίλοι, μνήcαcθε δὲ θούριδοc ἀλκῆc·
γιγνώcκω δ' ὅτι μοι πρόφρων κατένευcε Κρονίων
νίκην καὶ μέγα κῦδοc, ἀτὰρ Δαναοῖcί γε πῆμα·
νήπιοι, οἳ ἄρα δὴ τάδε τείχεα μηχανόωντο
ἀβλήχρ' οὐδενόcωρα· τὰ δ' οὐ μένοc ἀμὸν ἐρύξει·

Fig. 27: My antiquarian edition of the *Iliad*, The Parnassus Library of Greek and Latin Texts, Macmillan and Co., London/New York, 1897

Homer, books XX and XXI, *The Iliad: A New Prose Translation*, translated and with an introduction by Martin Hammond, Penguin, 1987

BAL DES AMBASSADEURS

Fig. 28

The best flea market in Buenos Aires is to be found in San Telmo. That is where I came across not only old volumes of the famous literary journal *Sur*, including an astounding edition from 1944, for which Borges had translated poems by Wallace Stevens and e.e. cummings, but also this yellowing postcard of an ambassadors' ball dating back to just before the war that would divide the ladies and gentlemen dancing in these festive surroundings, splitting them into hostile camps.

CIRCE

I purchased the Spanish edition of Alexander Pushkin's little book during a visit to the major Hermitage exhibition at the Prado, Madrid, in November 2011: *El viaje a Arzrum durante la campaña de 1829* (Editorial Minúscula, Barcelona, 2003). The original title was *Puteshestvie v Arzrum vo vremia pokhoda 1829 goda*. The introduction and translation into Spanish are by Selma Ancira.

As a young Russian rides with the regiments across that Slavic infinity, he keeps a diary, and he writes in such a way that readers almost two centuries later feel as if they themselves travelled with him. This is perhaps the secret: that writers can never know what detours their words will take, because whatever Pushkin might have imagined, it was surely not that another writer would come across his book in Spanish nearly two hundred years later at an exhibition in Madrid about the glories of his fallen empire.

HARBOUR

This map of the harbour of Mahon, Menorca, bears the following description: *El Puerto de Mahon y su costa, desde Cala Murta hasta Cala Rafalet, Ruinas del Castillo de Sn. Felipe, Baterias existentes y los Campamentos, Trincheras y Baterias del ultimo Sitio, grabado el Año de 1786 por Dn. Manl. Salvador Carmona, Grabador de S.M. y del Rey de Francia, Director en la Real Academia de Sn. Fernando. Escrito por Santo Drouët.* It is always strange to see an old map of a landscape that you know so intimately, complete with the fort, the bay and the harbour, and, where houses now stand, etched fields with pictures of little men who are occupied with their war and their siege, with trenches, batteries and all that other paraphernalia. What is missing from the 1786 map is the road I take almost every day, even though it would have come in very handy for those little sketched soldiers and their cannon.

Fig. 29

POSEIDON XVI

Details taken from the chapters on Whitman and Escoffier in Jonah Lehrer's curious and amazing book, *Proust Was a Neuroscientist*, Canongate Books, Edinburgh, 2011. Stravinsky, Cézanne, Woolf, George Eliot, all suffered from an exciting form of clairvoyance, which Lehrer analyses like a neurosurgeon. Being able to see things before others is a gift with serious consequences.

I gained the other knowledge from Wikipedia, the poet's resort in times of need.

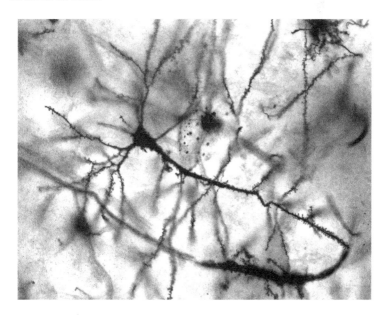

Fig. 30

HIPPOPOTAMUS

Fig. 31: Bar El Hipopótamo, corner of
Brasil/Defensa, San Telmo, Buenos Aires

HESIOD

Hesiod, *Theogony*, edited and translated by Glenn W. Most, Loeb
Classical Library, Harvard University Press, Cambridge/London, 2006

POSEIDON XVII

Leaving behind the cold and the height of Bogotá, you descend to
the coast. First the plane is not allowed to land because of an
apocalyptic storm, but then the pilot takes it shuddering down
anyway and suddenly you find yourself in the tropics. Some names
have something about them; they suck us in. I knew Cartagena,
on the dry coast of the Spanish southeast, but the tempting addition

Fig. 32

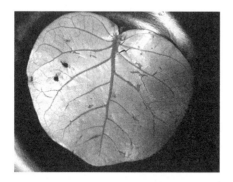

Fig. 33

of "de las Indias" is what did it. Tropical, old, colonial, a Spanish mirage in the distance, surrounded by ramparts you can walk
around, a small city clasped within her crenellated walls. And it was
from those walls that I saw the monument pointing towards the
lead-grey ocean, a wild flock of metallic birds, silhouetted against
the equally grey, menacing sky. The ramparts were meant to keep
out the British and the pirates; this city was repeatedly captured
and plundered. Founded in 1533 by Pedro de Heredia, it was one
of the first Spanish military bases in South America. From here,
the gold and magnificent golden works of art of the Zenú were
shipped to Spain to help finance Philip II's war against the Protestant
Netherlands—wasted gold. The poem is by the Colombian poet
Daniel Lemaitre Tono (1884–1961).

QUILOTOA

Fig. 34

ZOO

Jardin Zoológico, Plaza Italia, Buenos Aires

POSEIDON XVIII

Fig. 35: Kees van Dongen, *Self-portrait as Neptune*, 1922,
Centre Pompidou, Musée National d'Art Moderne, Paris

LIVES

Mémoires du Duc de Saint-Simon, Gallimard/Pléiade, Paris, 1983. There is an abridged version in three substantial volumes, *Memoirs: Duc de Saint-Simon*, translated by Lucy Norton, 1500 Books, New York, 2007. Together with Chateaubriand, this duke was one of Proust's intellectual forebears. Day after day, for more than thirty years, he recorded life at court in the Versailles of Louis XIV and Louis XV in his minuscule handwriting: intrigue, spite, privilege, war. An obsession with ranks and status, an incredibly sharp eye, still wonderful to read even today. There is no better cure for your own era than a merciless light thrown on individuals you can completely identify with, who lived in another period, one that has gone for good, people who were heading, slowly but surely, towards the revolution that would sweep them away in a raging storm.

BULL

In Colombia, bullfighting is a deadly business, and there are also those who protest. An article on the subject was published on July 1, 2011, in *El Tiempo*, Bogotá, accompanied by this photograph by Juan Pablo Rueda.

Fig. 36

POSEIDON XIX

Fig. 37

SISTERS

Fig. 38

For Charles Bonnet and Joseph Addison, see Arthur O. Lovejoy, *The Great Chain of Being: A Study of the History of an Idea*, Harvard University Press, 1936. I must have purchased and read the book years ago, because the notes in the margin are undeniably in my own handwriting. Where does everything go after we read it? Years ago, I underlined all manner of sentences, added exclamation marks, and some of that lost knowledge and wisdom must have seeped in somehow, and is now returning as a vague memory: the people quoted by Lovejoy, the English poet Joseph Addison and the Swiss Charles Bonnet, a physicist and philosopher who was one of the first to consider a theory of evolution, but who also believed in life after death. For years, the book slumbered in my Spanish house with the dogged patience of neglected books waiting for their time to come. Was it the letters formed by the worms on my white walls that led me back to the drowsing book in which a man calls a worm his sister? The secret pathways of the memory are labyrinthine and unfathomable.

WHALE

Details taken from the chapter "A Whale's End is the Beginning of Life at the Deep Seafloor" by Craig R. Smith, University of Hawaii, USA, in Clare Nouvian, *The Deep: The Extraordinary Creatures of the Abyss*, University of Chicago Press, Chicago, 2007.

BLUE

Classicist Anne Carson is one of the most interesting poets of our age. In the introduction to her book *Autobiography of Red*, she writes: "When Homer mentions blood, blood is *black*. When women appear,

Fig. 39

women are *neat-ankled* or *glancing*. Poseidon always has *the blue eyebrows of Poseidon.*" Just before that, she says, "What is an adjective? Nouns name the world. Verbs activate the names. Adjectives come from somewhere else. The word *adjective* (*epitheton* in Greek) is itself an adjective meaning 'placed on top', 'added', 'appended', 'foreign'. Adjectives seem fairly innocent additions, but look again. These small imported mechanisms are in charge of attaching everything in the world to its place in particularity. They are the latches of being."

Anne Carson, *Autobiography of Red. A Novel in Verse*, First Vintage Contemporaries Edition, Vintage Book, New York, 1999

POSEIDON XX

Heinrich Seuse, the Blessed Henry Suso, was one of the greatest German mystics, after Meister Eckhart. He lived in the fourteenth century and he wrote theological treatises and one of the first autobiographies in a remarkable early German. Borges, a master at tracking down influences of writers whom another writer could not have read, might even have seen Heidegger as a precursor to Seuse.

Just take a look at the language:
"Die Meister sprechen, Gott habe kein Wo, Er sei Alles im All. Nun tu die inneren Ohren deiner Seele auf und horche genau. Dieselben Meister sprechen auch in der Wissenschaft Logica, man komme zuweilen zur Kenntnis eines Dinges durch seinen Namen. Es spricht ein Lehrer, dass der Name 'Sein' der erste Name Gottes sei. So kehre deine Augen zu dem Sein in seiner lauteren Einfachheit, während du dies und das Teil-Sein fallen läßt. Nimm allein das Sein an sich selbst, das unvermischt ist mit Nichtsein; denn wie das Nichtsein

Fig. 40

alles Sein leugnet, also tut das Sein an sich, es leugnet alles Nichtsein. [. . .] Wie der göttlichen Personen Dreifalt bestehen kann in eines Seins Einigkeit, das kann niemand mit Worten vorbringen. Doch soviel man davon sprechen kann, daß der Vater ein Ursprung aller Gottheit des Sohnes und des Geistes sei, sowohl der Person wie dem Wesen nach [. . .]. Diese verborgenen Gedanken erschließt uns das klare Licht, der Lehrer Sankt Thomas, der spricht: Bei der Entgossenheit aus dem Herzen und der Vernunft des Vaters muß dies sein, daß Gott in seiner lichtreichen Erkenntnis mit einer Widerbeugung auf Sein göttliches Sein auf Sich Selbst blickt."

("The masters say that God has no Where, that He is everything in the universe. Now open the inner ears of your soul and listen attentively. Those same masters also say in the science of logic that one can sometimes gain knowledge of a thing through its name. A teacher says that the name 'existence' is the first name of God. Therefore turn your eyes towards existence in its pure simplicity, and abandon this or that partial existence. Take only existence in itself, which is unalloyed with non-existence, for as non-existence denies all existence, existence in itself denies all non-existence. [. . .] Nobody can express with words how the trinity of the Divine Persons can exist within the unity of one existence. But to the extent that one can talk about it, the Father is an origin of all the divinity of the Son and the Spirit, in terms of person as well as of essence [. . .]. These mysterious thoughts are made accessible to us by the clear light, the teacher Saint Thomas, who says: With the effusion from the heart and the mind of the Father, it must be that God in his luminous awareness gazes upon His own Self while bending down towards His divine existence.")

From: Walther Tritsch, *Christliche Geisteswelt*, Band II, *Die Welt der Mystik*, Verlag Werner Dausien, Hanau, 1986
Klaus Held, *Treffpunkt Platon*, Reclam, Stuttgart, 1990

WAR

Fig. 41

"Ik heb hier zó lang naartoe geleefd" ("I've waited so long for this day"),
interview with Katja Boonstra, in *de Volkskrant*, October 25, 2011

RATÓN

Fig. 42

Jaime Prats, "La extraña afición a los toros asesinos" ("The strange
passion for killer bulls"), *El País*, Madrid, August 21, 2011

POSIDONIA

Fig. 43

Albufera is the Spanish and *albuferra* the Menorcan word for an inland area of water, a lagoon.

Anthony Bonner, *Plants of the Balearic Islands*, Editorial Moll, Palma de Mallorca, 2005
Camí de Cavalls Guidebook, Fundació Desti, Menorca, 2010

POSEIDON XXI

Werner Heisenberg, *Physics and Philosophy*, Harper & Row Publishers, New York, 1962/Pelican Books, London, 1989
Die Vorsokratiker, translated and annotated by Jaap Mansveld, Reclam, Stuttgart, 1983
The quotes from Aristotle and Quintilian are from Glenn W. Most's translation of Hesiod's *Theogony* (see above).

OLD

Fig. 44

Written in Medellín, Colombia, summer 2011.

FLAME

There are risks associated with having educated friends, particularly when doubt sets in and you are in a place where it is impossible to check everything, and academic opinions on a subject differ. Was it in fact Pliny who maintained that Odysseus had not returned home after Circe? And yes, of course, the idea that Dante might not have read the *Odyssey* was a joke. No sooner had one of my friends received this piece than I was informed that in the Middle Ages there was extensive speculation that Odysseus had set off again on his travels after his return, speculation that may, or so I was told, have been prompted by a letter from Seneca to Lucilius, a letter I have been unable to track down. Another friend sent me back to the passage in the *Odyssey* where Tiresias advises Odysseus to leave again immediately after his return home, and to travel so far inland that no-one knows the purpose of the oar he has taken on his journey. However, travelling inland is not a sea journey and certainly not a voyage to the southern hemisphere. So I do not dare to put my hand in the fire for Pliny, even though he talks often enough about Odysseus. In the 53rd letter from Seneca to Lucilius I did find an indication that Odysseus was always seasick, which in itself is strange enough for an eternal sailor, but most likely intended to lend literary allure to Seneca's own seasickness on a journey to Naples. Another tip was that I could find a passage in Hans Blumenberg's *Die Legitimität der Neuzeit* that said Odysseus set off again on his travels after his return to Ithaca. In Dante himself, no matter how close I get to the text, I cannot read that in so many words, but it is not there literally in Blumenberg either, although he comes close. "Here we do not encounter the hero of Homer's legends, who met the danger of the Sirens, but an Odysseus whom Dante later developed and freely invented on the basis of his restless curiosity about the world—an Odysseus, *who does not return to Ithaca* [my italics], but who undertakes the ultimate adventure of crossing the borders of the known world, by sailing through the pillars of Hercules, and who, after a five-month journey across the ocean, is shipwrecked within sight of a mysterious mountain. Virgil and Dante meet the hero of antiquity in the eighth circle of hell among the flickering flames in the ditch of the false counsellors, and hear the story of his last journey from him." An intriguing detail here is that he drowned as punishment for the sin of *curiositas*—the theme of Blumenberg's book—but is punished in Hell as a deceiver because of the Trojan Horse.

Still, it gave me the experience of reading Blumenberg and some pleasant letters from friends, and the conclusion that it was not the heathen god Poseidon whose vengeance led to Odysseus' downfall, but the Christian god, lending his maritime colleague a helping hand.

Hans Blumenberg, *Die Legitimität der Neuzeit*, Vol. 3: "Der Prozess der theoretischen Neugierde," Suhrkamp, Frankfurt am Main, 1996
Dante Alighieri, *Divina Commedia*, with a Dutch translation by Frederica Bremer, H.D. Tjeenk Willink & Zoon nv, Haarlem, 1941
Dante Alighieri, *The Divine Comedy*, Italian text with translation and comment by John D. Sinclair, Oxford University Press, 1939; *Inferno*, Canto XXVI

POSEIDON XXII

Fig. 45: The temple of Segesta

Divers found this statue in 1926 off the coast by Cape Artemision on board a sunken ship from the first century B.C. Speculation surrounds the statue, as some scholars believe it represents Zeus, rather than Poseidon. The fingers closed in that elegant gesture may once have held a trident, or perhaps a thunderbolt.

Homer, *The Odyssey*, Book I, translated by E. V. Rieu, revised by his son D. C. Rieu in consultation with Dr Peter V. Jones, Penguin Books, 1946/1991

Fig. 46: Poseidon of Cape Artemision, or Artemision Bronze, northern Euboea, *c.* 460 B.C., 209 centimetres

COLLEAGUES

Fig. 47: *Stauroteuthis syrtensis*

These details are from Claire Nouvian's marvellous book *The Deep: The Extraordinary Creatures of the Abyss*, University of Chicago Press, Chicago, 2007.

STONE

Fig. 48

The following books were significant for the writing of *Letters to Poseidon*:

Caroline Alexander, *The War That Killed Achilles*, Faber & Faber, London, 2010

Klaus Held, *Treffpunkt Platon, Philosophischer Reiseführer durch die Länder des Mittelmeers*, Reclam, Stuttgart, 1990

Samuel IJsseling, *Apollo, Dionysos, Aphrodite en de anderen*, Boom, Amsterdam, 1994

Michael Jacobs, *Andes*, Granta Books, London, 2010

Alberto Manguel, *Homer's* The Iliad *and* The Odyssey, Atlantic Books, London, 2007

Jean Seznec, *Das Fortleben der antiken Götter*, Wilhelm Fink Verlag, Munich, 1990

Jean-Pierre Vernant, *Mythe et pensée chez les Grecs*, La Découverte/ Brosché, Paris, 1996

Other books I have referred to are listed in the notes on that chapter.

The Wallace Stevens epigraph comes from the poem "Notes Toward a Supreme Fiction."

ACKNOWLEDGEMENTS

A book that wilfully spins off in all kinds of different directions, taking in the depths of the oceans and the lofty heights of the gods, is sure to present the author with quite a few unexpected problems. Fortunately, there are friends who know the answers to difficult questions, and who can advise and assist the author on his quest through the real and the invisible world. I would like to mention some of those friends by name, so that I may thank them. They were Pedro Alejo Gómez, Helga van Beuningen, Robbert Dijkgraaf, Wolther Kassies, Antje Landshoff-Ellermann, Emilia Lodigiani, Alberto Manguel, Fik Meijer, David Rijser, Julius Roos, Hans Roters, Rüdiger Safranski and Peter Sloterdijk. At Suhrkamp publishing house, Julia Ketterer, Matthias Reiner and Katja Bohlmann for their work on the text and the pictures, and finally Simone Sassen and Susanne Schaber, who have followed the project for four years, from start to finish.

C.N.

PICTURE CREDITS

CEES NOOTEBOOM was born in The Hague in 1933, and now lives in Amsterdam and on the island of Menorca. He is a poet, a novelist and a travel writer whose books include *Rituals* (1983), *The Following Story* (1994), *Roads to Santiago* (1997), *All Souls' Day* (2001), *The Foxes Come at Night* (2011) and *Roads to Berlin* (2012). He has been awarded the Dutch Literature Prize and for *Roads to Berlin* he received the German Order of Merit.

LAURA WATKINSON is a translator from Dutch, Italian and German, including works by Jan van Mersbergen, Tonke Dragt and Peter Terrin. She lives in Amsterdam.